Collectibles 101™:

BASEBALL

Don Raycraft, Michael Raycraft & RC Raycraft

Schiffer Publishing Ltd®
4880 Lower Valley Road, Atglen, PA 19310 USA

DEDICATION

For Scott

Library of Congress Catalog Card Number: 98-89304

Designed by Bonnie M. Hensley
Layout by Randy L. Hensley
Type set in Windsor BT/Korinna BT

ISBN: 0-7643-0759-2
Printed in China
1 2 3 4

Published by Schiffer Publishing Ltd.
4880 Lower Valley Road
Atglen, PA 19310
Phone: (610) 593-1777; Fax: (610) 593-2002
E-mail: Schifferbk@aol.com
Please visit our web site catalog at
www.schifferbooks.com

This book may be purchased from the publisher.
Include $3.95 for shipping. Please try your bookstore first.
We are interested in hearing from authors
with book ideas on related subjects.
You may write for a free printed catalog.

In Europe, Schiffer books are distributed by
Bushwood Books
6 Marksbury Avenue
Kew Gardens
Surrey TW9 4JF England
Phone: 44 (0)181 392-8585; Fax: 44 (0)181 392-9876
E-mail: Bushwd@aol.com

Contents

Foreword

I began collecting sports memorabilia in March 1980. I was 10 years old and my family traveled to Indianapolis to meet Pete Rose, who had recently been traded by the Reds to the Phillies. That afternoon stands out in my mind because the location where Pete was scheduled to appear changed 3 times, and when the family station wagon arrived at the appointed Holiday Inn we were greeted by Pete's double-parked Rolls Royce leaking oil in the hotel valet area.

Since that afternoon I have attended hundreds of card shows throughout the United States and had the opportunity to mingle with sports legends ranging from Michael Jordan to someone claiming to be Walt Dropo's brother.

As time passed appreciation for my own collection has changed:

- An autographed Darrell Evans program brings back memories of a family trip to the All-Star game at old Comiskey Park in 1983.

- A menu signed by Ted Williams reminds me of a special meal I had the summer after I graduated from high school.

- A horse-racing program autographed by baseball Hall of Famer Albert Chandler is reminiscent of a great afternoon spent at the Keeneland track while a student at the University of Kentucky.

- A game-worn (& bloodstained) University of Illinois basketball jersey is significant because I bought it for my girlfriend to impress her when we first started dating.

The point is that values come and go as quickly as Ron Kittle's career did in 1984. Those who purchase Hartland Statues or Babe Ruth Underwear Boxes for financial gain would be better off investing in government bonds or T-bills.

The "value" to be gained from the Hobby are the memories one associates with the experience. The recollections of the time so-and-so threw up in the car on the way to meet Hank Aaron or that summer trip to the Baseball Hall of Fame have helped me through some of life's darkest moments. For that alone, I am grateful.

I am also grateful to my parents whose bankroll and station wagon helped to instill the "thrill of the hunt" in me at an early age. I learned early on that it's the finding—not the buying—that is the key. In more recent years, my wife has joined the pursuit. Her enthusiasm and willingness to display autographed Enos Slaughter photos above her fireplace revitalized my interest in the hobby. Thank you.

The primary goal of *Baseball Collectibles 101* is to provide basic insider information to the novice collector. If our advice results in a few anecdotes, legends, or memories along the way, we will have completed our task.

Michael Raycraft
December 1998

Acknowledgments

The authors sincerely appreciate the assistance, direction, opinions, and friendship of the individuals listed below. Their contributions have made this project especially meaningful to us.We are in their debt.

Dr. Craig Bazzani
Dick Dobbins
Pete Del Signore
Dave Fyliepek
Jim Doherty
Lou Hagenbruch
Emily Raycraft
Stew Salowitz
John Rose
Craig Holly
Dr. Loren Logsdon
Bill Striegel
Dr. Steve Epperson
Ron Roop
Matt Bazzani
Aaron Green
Ross Bartels
Doug Bartels
Bill Walter
Craig Walter
Jeff Ellish
Mike Bazzani
Alex Hood
Doug Congdon-Martin
Wayne Otto
Dr. David Darnall
Bill Draper
Sport Palmer
David Faulkner
Alan Weintraub Esq.
Gary Willis Esq.
Lanny Lobdell
Rick Wayne Esq.
Bobby Farling
Kim Lorraine
Radar Dirks
Tanya Uphoff
Preston Boyd
Dorcas Salowitz
Dale Troyer
David Bertshe
Miles Bertshe
Carol Raycraft
Kevin Ellis
Jeff Brumleve
Dr. John Dillon
Sam Rudgard
Irving Azoff
Joe Walsh
Nicholas Tedesco
Molly Higgins
Cyril Zoerner
Ron Guthoff
Mike North
Jack Frisch
David Davis
Tim Pittman
Kelly Block
Steve Straub

Photography

Dick Dobbins
Scott Raycraft
Lou Hagenbruch
Don Raycraft
Walter Carter II

Contributors

Dick Dobbins

Author, collector, educator, memorabilia dealer, opera buff, and one of the most respected experts in the field of sports memorabilia with specialties in the areas of uniforms, autographs, and the Pacific Coast League.

Lou Hagenbruch

Hartland collector since 1958 with a complete run of original baseball statues from Wisconsin, Dallas, and Missouri. M.S. from the University of Illinois and a two sport athlete at McKendree College.

Lanny Lobdell

Retired Internal Revenue agent and lifelong Chicago Cub fan (and periodic foe). Sometime rightfielder for Octavia High School in Central Illinois in the late 1950s. Graduate of Illinois Wesleyan University.

Dr. Loren Logsdon

English professor at Eureka College with a doctorate from Ohio University. Collector of Ethan Allen All-Star Baseball games since 1948. Exceptional 3-point shooter.

Stew Salowitz

Stew Salowitz is the sports information director at Illinois Wesleyan University in Bloomington, Illinois. His motorcycle license plate reads "CHILI 3". He is the author of five books.

Introduction

At a point in time when professional football and basketball did not exist, major league baseball had already been America's pastime for more than sixty years. Forgotten nineteenth century legends like Mickey Welch, Cap Anson, George Davis, Sam Thompson, and Charles Radbourn were national heroes long before Dr. James Naismith joined the Springfield YMCA.

Baseball kranks or fanatics looked upon a trip to the ball yard to see King Kelly and Jesse "The Crab" Burkett almost as a religious pilgrimage. If they purchased a program or a picture of their hero, it became a treasured family artifact of a memorable excursion to see the Brooklyn Atlantics, Providence Grays, or Cleveland Naps. These long-gone kranks became the first collectors and "keepers" of baseball memorabilia.

Hopefully, some of the information in this volume will assist today's collectors in emulating that first generation of baseball fanatics or "bugs" and, with luck, maybe we will find some of the treasures they left behind a century ago.

The authors sincerely believe that the baseball collectible or antique that you are seeking is still out there. We have bought items ranging from a 1934 St. Louis Browns jersey to "blankets" of Joe Jackson and Ty Cobb in basements and at flea markets for a fraction of their value. We have also made a hundred fruitless trips in search of something that was probably never there.

We are absolutely convinced that there is an unopened case of 1953 Topps baseball cards in the basement of an abandoned country store or drug store somewhere in the middle of central Illinois. The trick is to find it.

We hope the basement is still dry when we do.

Chapter 1

Why Baseball?

By Lanny Lobdell

Several summers ago while driving home from Chicago after a rare Cubs' victory, a friend and I had a two-hour discussion on why baseball is the greatest game and will always be America's pastime.

We came to the conclusion that not only is baseball the greatest game, it is the perfect game. Even though greedy owners, selfish players, and arrogant umpires have joined forces in an attempt to ruin the sport, the concept of baseball and the game itself remain close to perfection.

On that July evening we must have come up with 100 reasons why baseball is the greatest game. Below I have provided an abridged list.

- It is the only major American team sport without a clock.
- Twenty-seven outs are as difficult to get today as they were when Amos Rusie and Eddie Plank were mound legends. The last out is still the toughest, and that's why the closers are paid millions of dollars for pitching 52 innings a season.
- It is the only American major team sport played in the summer, the best season.
- If the distance between home and first base was 89', it would have been a foot too short, and 91' would have been a foot too long. Think about it. If the bases had been 91' apart, there would be too many 1-0 and 2-1 games. The distance was perfect in 1901 and it will be perfect in 2001.
- It is the only game where century-old facts and statistics are still important. Everyone knows Ruth hit 60 homeruns in 1927 and that Maris hit 61 in 1961. Why do 30,000 fans come to the game two hours early to see Mark McGwire take batting practice? Does anyone know (or care) how many touchdowns Red Grange scored for the Bears?
- Baseball records are precise. In football, if Jim Brown gained 8 feet it went into the records as 3 yards. Baseball fans know that Bill Mazerowski beat the Yankees in the seventh game of the 1960 World Series with a homerun off of Ralph Terry. How many fans know who played in the 1960 NBA finals or the Rose Bowl?
- Baseball can be played professionally by someone who isn't 6'11" or weighs in excess of 300 pounds. In other words, it could be played at the highest level by someone like you or a younger version of me. Greg Maddux can put on his glasses and a hat and walk through any shopping mall in Atlanta. Can Shaq or Reggie White duplicate that feat without being mobbed?
- Baseball is a cerebral game enjoyed best by those endowed with the ability and desire to think for themselves. Baseball is like war with all the strategy and planning of battle. That's why Don Zimmer, an all-time great third base coach, was less successful as a manager. Zimmer was quoted once as saying he didn't care about statistics, his emphasis was on his instincts. As a coach, where decisions are made instantly, he was usually correct. Gut feelings are okay in picking horses or sending in a runner from third in the ninth inning, but not in making calculated moves on the chessboard of baseball.
- Baseball is a sport where even the worst team will beat the best team in the league one out of three games. Your team, no matter how bad, has a legitimate chance to win on the one day of the year when you choose to attend the game.
- It is not necessarily the best team that wins a particular game, it often is the luckiest team that wins. Luck plays a vital role in baseball because of the huge playing area. It doesn't make any difference if it's luck or skill, baseball is unpredictable and always exciting.
- From a father/son bonding standpoint, nothing can beat baseball. It might be the same for the mother/daughter relationship, but I can't be sure.

The Day I Rediscovered Mickey Mantle

By Don Raycraft

When the 1953 baseball cards first came out, I was in the twilight of a mediocre career as a grade school student with junior high looming on the horizon. I made my purchases a pack at a time with the nickel my father gave his only son for "something to chew on" each school day. When there were no feared seventh graders sitting on their bikes in front of DeMent's Grocery on Oakland Avenue in Bloomington, Illinois, I fearlessly shuffled inside, cast a quick glance at the new Esquire magazine on the rack and ordered my daily pack. A few of my friends liked Camels, but I was weak for Topps.

I was a Yankee fan (krank, bug) and there were twenty cards to find in 1953. Alphabetically, they ranged from Yogi Berra to Gene Woodling. Athletically, they ranged from Mickey Mantle to Art Schult. Art's Yankee career was limited to no hits and three runs scored. Mickey was a bit more successful. In addition to 536 more homeruns, he scored 1674 more runs than Art.

Baseball cards in 1953 had no intrinsic value other than to periodically trade or put in your bicycle spokes. The biggest swap I ever consummated was the following:

Yankees: Mantle, Carey, Reynolds, Silvera, and Martin
for
Browns: Dyck, Harrist, Fannin, Pillette, and Wertz.

It took a week to negotiate it, but finally the deal was completed. Bill Veeck and George Weiss would have been proud, though George would have probably been a hell of a lot more proud than Bill.

I loved the Mantle card so much that I pinned it to my bulletin board so I could look at it while I was studying. In retrospect, I didn't see it much.

At some point my collection was lost, thrown away, or burned. About 15 years ago, I found in my mother's attic an old copy of Esquire from 1954. The bookmark was still in place near the centerfold. It was my Mantle card with the pin hole.

It was my best day in baseball.

Chapter 2

Uniforms & Equipment

Finding and purchasing a major league game-worn jersey or game-used bat is not difficult and can be accomplished with relatively little effort. The challenge becomes a little more complex and considerably more costly if the player has led the league in batting, wins, or homeruns.

The uniforms and bats of common players are not in great demand and are available at reasonable prices in quantity. When you purchase the bat or jersey of a reserve catcher from Pittsburgh or the fifth outfielder from the Brewers, you can be assured that it is probably legitimate because there is not enough interest or potential profit to reproduce or fake it. Other than his family and friends, very few people care.

When you begin your quest for the jersey or bat of a more prominent player, the situation becomes a little more cloudy and certainly more costly. A Cal Ripken game-used bat would cost about $1,000 2,000 if you could find a legitimate example. A Billy Ripken bat is still out there for $50-75 with few takers. Anything from Cal is going to have to be rigorously examined to insure its authenticity. Anything from Billy is almost certainly legitimate.

Notes on Collecting Uniforms & Equipment

1. Minor and major league game-worn uniforms are available in large quantities from dealers who are specialists in the field. Almost all have extensive catalogs (see Sources).
2. The long term investment possibilities of most "common" player jerseys are minimal. The jerseys ($35–125) should be purchased to be worn, enjoyed, or hung on a wall.
3. Several major league teams have yearly "garage sales" where they sell uniforms and equipment directly to their fans. Prices tend to be slanted toward the exceedingly high retail. There are few bargains but authenticity is usually not much of a problem.
4. Jerseys of contemporary "star" or "superstar" players have reached the price plateau that makes it economically rewarding to "fake" them with seemingly correct tagging and signs of use and then offer them for sale to collectors. If you spend $500 to $2,000 for a game-worn "star" jersey, make it a point to secure a written and detailed description and a provenance of the jersey. This should go way beyond a simple certificate of authenticity. If you have the slightest question about the jersey, *don't buy it*.
5. Game jerseys worn by members of the Hall of Fame start about $1,200 (Don Sutton, Phil Niekro) and extend into six figures. Hire a respected outside authority to examine the jersey before you purchase it. It is money well spent.
6. An increasing number of players have contractual control over their uniforms and bats rather than allowing them to be furnished by their teams. This means you have to deal with the player's agent or representative directly to acquire a jersey or other game-used equipment.

Q & A with Wayne Otto

Wayne Otto of Pro-Am Sports & Memorabilia has been in the game-worn uniforms and equipment business for 17 years and has done over 50 bulk purchases from professional teams. He lists over 7,000 game-worn items in his catalog. Pro-Am Sports can be reached at:

P.O. Box 2628
Boone, North Carolina 28607

From the standpoint of an investment, do you see "common" player jerseys increasing in price over the next decade?

"Common" player jerseys from the 1960s back, and in some cases and styles the 1970s, are increasing in value and some are even skyrocketing. A lot of collectors want certain styles, and this creates escalating prices.

What do you think of the "Turn Back the Clock" jerseys?

They're nice and it gives collectors more styles and varieties to collect.

What player jerseys that you have had have been the easiest to sell?

Some collectors collect uniforms of players that have played at a certain college or try to get an example of a player's uniform with all the teams for whom he played. No one player sells better than an other.

What team jerseys are the most popular among collectors?

Most of the old established teams like the New York Knicks, New York Giants, Philadelphia Eagles, Boston Red Sox, and New York Yankees.

Which team has jerseys that are the most difficult to sell?

A losing team from an era with ugly uniforms such as the 1980s Cleveland Cavaliers or the 1980s Houston Astros are a tough sell.

When you buy jerseys directly from a team do you have to buy everything or can you pick and choose?

I buy everything in a bulk purchase. I don't want to pick and choose and they don't either.

Why are the Yankee jerseys so hard to find for sale?

The Yankees just don't let anything out. Collectors very rarely see them for sale.

Is there much interest in minor league jerseys?

Because of their relatively low prices and team names and logos, minor league jerseys are taking off in the hobby.

What is the single rarest baseball jersey you have offered for sale?

Probably a 1957 Milwaukee Braves Wes Covington road jersey with the tomahawk style. It was a really nice shirt.

Which major league baseball team jerseys are the most difficult to acquire?

It changes from ownership to ownership. The New York Yankees, Toronto Blue Jays, and Detroit Tigers have probably been the toughest over the years.

Which are the least difficult major league jerseys to buy?

Several teams seem to sell their game gear every year. Atlanta, Texas, Houston, and Pittsburgh all fall into this category.

What should a collector look for or demand when purchasing the jersey of a Reggie Jackson, Mike Schmidt, Cal Ripkin, Jr. or other players at the "superstar" level?

The source is number one. If somebody is going to try to "fake" a jersey, it will be of a star. Of course, be sure to check for game wear, proper tagging, stitching, numbers, and letter spacing.

How much does repair, like replacing a number, a name on the back, or logo on a jersey affect its price?

Repairs on football jerseys are usually good. They show the jersey was used. Number changes and name changes...on baseball jerseys somewhat devalue them. A lot of teams send some of their jerseys to the minor leagues for use or use them with their expanded rosters in spring training and that is when a lot of the changes take place.

Q & A with Dick Dobbins

Dick Dobbins has lived in northern California his entire life. He spent 32 years as a teacher, coach, and public school administrator. He is the author of the best selling history of the Pacific Coast League, *Nuggets on the Diamond* and *The Grand Minor League—An Oral History of the Pacific Coast League*. Dobbins has been a collector of baseball memorabilia since 1946 and is on a short list of the most respected and renowned individuals in the field. He recently served as a consultant for the HBO documentary on Joe DiMaggio.

How did you get interested in collecting baseball memorabilia?

I was about twelve years old and really wanted a hat from the San Francisco Seals or the Oakland Oaks which were both our local teams. You could always get the souvenir hats but that wasn't quite the same thing as one that had been worn in a game. Occasionally, a ballplayer would give you one of his cracked bats and I would always try to get the whole team to sign the bat. That was kind of my early start in collecting baseball memorabilia. My first real breakthrough was answering an advertisement and picking up a Washington Senators jersey from 1969 for $30. The Senators' jersey was my first and it absolutely hooked me. To be able to come up with something that had actually been worn by a player in a major league game was a thrill. Who could have asked for anything more?

Over the years, what was your greatest find?

There have been lots of great finds. For example, I found a Pirates flannel uniform with a number like 43 or another high number on the back but you could see the outline of a 9, 8, 6, or 3 and, of course, I got lucky and it was Willie Stargel's #8. By the way, when you restore a jersey, take pictures before you begin the restoration process so you have a photographic record of what has happened to the jersey. This makes it quite obvious that you are not pulling some kind of con game which, sadly, is something we have to consider in this day and age. The most joyful find for me was when a former Pacific Coast League player gave me a call and said that he had a guy that had a uniform he wanted to sell. It was a gray jersey that had "Norfolk" and a #53 on the back. It also had some stitching in the collar that said "DiMaggio", so I went out and purchased this jersey. It was a DiMaggio Yankee jersey that had been sent down to their minor league team in Norfolk, Virginia. The new numbers had stained the jersey pretty heavily, but with a lot of care and diluted bleach and a tooth brush, I was able to restore it to a good solid piece and put "New York" on it. I could see the imprint from the past and a number 5 on the back. I came up with the prettiest uniform that was obviously DiMaggio's and it was very difficult to tell that it had been restored.

Are there any special memorabilia shows that you don't want to miss each year?

This is an easy question for me to answer but it may not be as easy for other collectors. Out here on the West Coast, we do not have a great many shows anyway. We do have one of the best regional shows on Labor Day that is now sponsored by Tri-Star. Over the past 20 years, we have had a marvelous Labor Day show, but we had politics take over and economic wars with one show confronting another one. I think we have worked that down now to one sponsor of one show on that weekend.

The real answer to that question is the National Sports Convention. There's a lot wrong with the National, but there is the annual meeting of old friends that you do not see elsewhere. There are a lot of good regional shows, but if you can attend only one show, the National is probably the one. It moves each year from city to city.

If you were going to start collecting baseball memorabilia today, in what area would you be the most interested?

I think that's an economic question more than anything else. If I were a young person in my twenties, I would start collecting bats. The one thing you have to do is to gain enough knowledge to know what you are doing because in every field there is a lot of deception that is always going on. I think it is harder to do that with bats if you know some basic ground rules, so you can acquire bats of very good players for not a lot of money. With Lou Gehrig jerseys going for $180,000 and other uniforms for mega-dollars, bats look like pretty good investments. You can pick up a Larry Walker bat for under $100 and there are a lot of good players still out there at reasonable prices. Some people are collecting gloves today, but I would be very careful because I think gloves are not a wise move because of all the duplicity that is going on. I would never collect hats of stars because anybody can go down to the corner sporting goods store and buy a cap and write a number under the brim and it is almost impossible to tell the real from the fake. The caps are identical.

What pieces over the years that you have sold, do you have the most regret about not keeping?

That question is pretty easy to answer. In 1992 I sold most of my collection of uniforms and memorabilia to Leland's in New York City and I was a firm believer that everything had to go. I couldn't "cherry pick" because that was not fair to them. There were a few items I was really sorry to see go. One of them was a ball from one of the New York Giants World Series games in the early 1920s. It was from the George Kelly estate. It was a ball that Kelly held on to after an out to end one of the games. He kept the ball and it was very dirty. It was back from when they used only a few balls during a game and it was signed by the manager, somebody named McGraw, and the coach, somebody named Hughie Jennings, and then by each of the nine players. The nine players included Kelly, Frank Frisch, Travis Jackson, and Ross Youngs. It also listed the final score of the game. Youngs is almost an impossible autograph because he died very young. Another piece I regretted selling was an old political ad that ran in Harper's Monthly. It was a large artist's rendering of Abraham Lincoln and he was going to bat with his challengers like Stephen Douglas. It was framed and I found it in an antiques shop in San Francisco and just really fell in love with it. It hung on my wall for a short time before it went east to Leland's. That was something I was sorry to see go.

What is the single best piece of baseball memorabilia that you have owned?

Probably my favorite piece is Albert Spalding's book, *Baseball That Had Been,* owned by George Washington Bradley. Bradley threw the first no-hitter in the history of major league baseball. Bradley started his big league career in 1876. This book was inscribed from Bradley to his grandson. Sadly, when I got it, the book was a total shambles so I had to spend a lot of money to have it restored. This is something that collectors should realize. There is really nothing wrong with restoration. You are doing your hobby a real service by bringing a tattered piece of memorabilia back to life. The one thing that you must remember when you restore a piece is that you do it accurately and you don't make little changes. Changes that turn a piece from a "rookie" that doesn't make the team to a hall of famer are just downright criminal.

What about letters of authenticity?

The old concept of getting a letter of authenticity is a joke. If somebody is going to fake a uniform or autograph, what's the problem with faking a letter of authenticity to go along with it? The one thing that has probably saved me thousands of dollars over the years was the old saying "When in doubt, punt." If you have any questions about something, it is not even worth picking up. If you have a question today, are you going to have that same question five years from now? Taking a very conservative path is the best thing you can do in purchasing any uniform or piece of baseball memorabilia.

If you were looking for the autograph of some of the nineteenth century greats, where would you begin the search?

That's a tough question especially if you live out on the West Coast. Most of the sources of that type of material are on the East Coast. The concept again of the letter of authenticity again is meaningless. You have to know who you are buying it from. Forty years ago, there was a man in Brooklyn who bought old books and cut up the borders and used the paper to fake autographs. They still turn up in auctions all the time. If you are careful, you will save yourself a lot of money.

Are there any publications that you feel are essential for baseball memorabilia collectors?

Dennis Purdy's *Vintage and Classic Baseball Collector* is a very good magazine. Purdy calls things the way he sees them. He is not your typical writer. Each issue has articles about a myriad of topics that are analyzed in depth. It is a keeper, a very good publication.

If you are going to be a collector, you have to take *Sports Collectors Digest*. It's got lots of ads and has both reputable dealers and shady dealers. A lot of people criticize *SCD* because they won't take a stand on controversial issues because they are afraid of being sued, and that's probably a legitimate concern at this point. If you are looking for good items, it is at least a way to be aware of their existence and availability. The paper comes out weekly and it's completely impossible to digest everything that goes on through *SCD*.

Insights from Dick Dobbins on Uniform & Bat Collecting

Serious collectors should focus on flannels. It is much more difficult to find flannels, but considerably easier to determine if they are real.

One of the problems collectors face with knit jerseys is that they are so easy to fake. You can go to a local sporting goods store and pick up a blank jersey and get creative or buy a replica jersey and do anything you want with it to make it appear to be what it isn't.

It is important to keep in mind when you collect game-worn major league uniforms that there is a great deal of inconsistency in the manufacturing and the tagging of jerseys. The most consistent thing you will encounter is the constant inconsistency. When you find a jersey, if you have the slightest question about it, do some research and be convinced it is "right" before you buy it. The key is to buy intellectually and not emotionally.

With the coming of knit jerseys in the early 1970s many teams went to name plates on the back of the jerseys rather than individually lettering each one. This allowed jerseys to be quickly recycled when one name plate was taken off and another one added. The name plate also made it simpler to put the name of a star player on a plate to "fake" a jersey.

You can often learn more about a jersey from the inside of it than from the outside. Turn the jersey inside out and see if you find any stitch marks or nicks that have no reason to be there. Hold the jersey up to the light and see if there are any stains or shadows of numbers or letters that have been removed or replaced.

Bats

There are four categories of bats that are of interest to collectors.

1. Game-used bats—A bat actually used in a game. Two common terms used to describe game-used bats in advertisements are "UC" and "C". "UC" refers to a game-used bat that is uncracked. "C" refers to a game-used bat that has been cracked. Game bats are always uncracked because they have never been used.
2. Game bat—A bat designed for use in a game but never used. The game bat is exactly the same bat as the game-used bat but never made it into action.
3. Retail or store-bought bat—A bat manufactured to be sold in a sporting goods store to the general public. Often these bats are made to different standards of quality than the bat designed for the professional player.

4. Commemorative bats—A bat produced for sale as a collectible and not as a game bat. Commemorative bats usually celebrate an individual's career or a historical moment in baseball history. These bats are generally produced in limited quantities and numbered editions. The Cooperstown Bat Company and the Hall of Fame have numerous commemorative bats for sale in their catalogs. The Hall of Fame induction bat offered each year is an example of a commemorative bat that is eagerly collected because of its quality and limited production (1,000).

Notes on Collecting Bats

Major league teams typically pay about $30 each for their bats. After they have been used and broken collectors pay considerably more.

The black Sharpie is the pen of choice for autographing most bats. On black or very dark bats use a silver or gold paint pen. If possible, have the player sign near his stamped signature on the barrel of the bat if it is to be a single-signed example.

The Louisville Slugger name on a bat dates it from 1980 or later. Prior to that date the Hillerich and Bradsby name was used. "Flame Tempered" or "Flame Treated" is often found on sporting goods or retail bats. "Powerized" is used on many major league bats manufactured by Louisville Slugger.

On the Saturday morning (8 a.m.) of the Hall of Fame Induction Weekend in Cooperstown, 500 commemorative bats honoring that year's inductees go on sale in the gift shop. Lines usually begin to form several hours prior to the opening depending on who is being inducted. George Brett and Nolan Ryan draw much longer lines than Don Sutton and Larry Doby.

Sporting goods or retail bats of popular or Hall of Fame players from the 1920s–1950s are highly collectible. The condition of the bats and the level of stardom of the player dictates its values.

The value of a game-used bat can vary from $15 to $50,000 depending on its original owner, condition, and the documentation or provenance that accompanies it.

If a bat has a team name ("Yankees" or "Cardinals") on the barrel rather than an individual player, it was purchased by the team for general use rather than for a specific player.

Sports Collectors Digest often contains detailed ads from dealers with lengthy lists of game-used bats for sale. The dealers listed in the Sources section of this book also have large quantities of bats bought directly form the teams.

Selected "Buy" Prices of Game-Used Hall of Fame Jerseys and Bats

A "buy" price is the amount a dealer will pay for a given item. The buy price could almost be considered a wholesale price because the dealer will mark the piece up before offering it for sale again. We have chosen ten Hall of Fame players whose names have appeared in advertisements from dealers wanting to "buy" their game-worn flannel jerseys and game-used baseball bats. It is assumed that the jerseys and bats have not been altered in any way.

	Game-Worn Flannel Jersey	Game-Used Bat
Hank Aaron	$7,000	$2,500
Richie Ashburn	$6,000	$1,500
Ernie Banks	$7,500	$1,500
Roy Campanella	$10,000	$3,000
Ty Cobb	$45,000	$15,000
Eddie Collins	$10,000	$2,500
Jimmie Fox	$20,000	$3,500
Rogers Hornsby	$10,000	$2,000
Reggie Jackson	$2,000	$700
Eddie Mathews	$6,000	$1,200

The Oldest Baseball

The "Fly Creek" baseball was found in a trunk in a village just north of Cooperstown and became a cornerstone of the Hall of Fame collection. In a 1915 issue of *Baseball Magazine,* the following brief article appeared about another early baseball:

> The oldest baseball in existence is owned by the president of the East Church Baseball League of Pittsburgh. The ball is nearly fifty-three years old. It was used first in a championship game of Newburgh, NY. The game was played on June 20, 1862, and ended 49-18 in favor of the Kingston team."
>
> The ball carries $500 burglary insurance and $500 fire insurance. It was given to its present owner by John Miller, who played first base on the Eclipse team. Miller is 100 years old now and lives in Cornwell-on-the-Hudson.

Hopefully, the present owner has increased his or her homeowner's insurance to cover the enhanced value of the baseball.

Flannel Detroit Tigers jersey, Nolen "Cliff" Richardson. No number on the back, extra long sleeve (sometimes even below the elbow), thread stitching in the back tail (lower right). The jersey dates from 1929, and the "3" is possibly indicative of his position—first base.The early jerseys were done primarily by Rawlings in St. Louis. They are thick and heavy, and hard to price because they don't turn up very often, $1500–2000.

Lou Gehrig's 1931 Japan Tour jersey. The logo is faded, name embroidered into the tail, with #4 on the back, heavy, made by Rawlings, sold by the Gehrig family for $55,000. One of the finest and rarest Gehrig jerseys ever located. If this was going to be auctioned today it could easily bring $125,000.

Gehrig home jersey. The name is in the collar, and the jersey is in excellent shape, with pinstripe, NY logo, and longer sleeves. $100,000 plus. Jersey collecting is a lot like playing the stock market because prices are constantly going up and down.

Eddie Joost's 1947 Philadelphia A's road jersey, clean tagged with name and year. Different teams are scarcer than others and old A's flannels are rare. $1800–2200

Plain Detroit Tiger jersey of Hall of Famer Charlie Gehringer, with name chain-stitched on a piece of felt and then stitched to the collar, made by Wilson. $5000

St. Louis Browns jersey of Hall of Famer Rogers Hornsby. Patch on sleeve, name in the collar, pullover style with half button-down. $8000–10,000

Hal Trosky Cleveland Indians pinstripe road jersey. Dated 1938, it is a scarce style. $1500–2000

Don Gutteredge Browns home jersey, 1945 season. Rawlings pull-over style, shadow effect on the numbers, WWII shield on sleeve. $800–1000

Wilson Cleveland Indian jersey, Jack Salverson. Size 46 with WWII shield on sleeve. $700–1000

Don Heffner's 1943 road jersey, St. Louis Browns. $800–1000

Ned Garver, 1952, restored. "Browns" replaced after trip to minor leagues. Patch on sleeve. $1000–1300

Restored Wilson Joe DiMaggio, sent to Norfolk, Virginia, changed to #53. In a restoration project such as this it is essential to keep a photographic record of each step in the process. If this jersey was held up to a window on a sunny day you could see the previous marking of New York with the stitch holes. After the lettering and numbers are removed more pictures are taken. The numbers often have bled into the flannel over time. A light mixture of bleach and water can be utilized with a toothbrush to blend the colors back to the gray and provide a consistent look to the jersey. A "real" Joe DiMaggio jersey would probably sell for $85,000–100,000 at auction. A restored jersey takes a heavy reduction in price because it is a "manipulated" jersey. The letter of authenticity that went with the jersey when it was sold at Leland's was accompanied by the photographs that spelled out each and every step of the restoration process. This jersey was restored and not changed. There is a major difference.

Davey Williams New York Giants 1951 World Series road jersey, flannel. $1000

Pirates vest-style home jersey, late 1960s, #45, Rawlings tag. $600–$800

Oakland A's 1969 Hank Bauer, Pacific misty green lettering and number, size 48, no name on the back. $500–700

1971 Vida Blue jersey, Oakland A's. California gold, size 42, name on the back. $1,000–$1,200

1969 Rollie Fingers vest-style A's jersey, #34. $1300–1800

1965 Senators road jersey, flannel. $700

Whitey Lockman, 1962 common San Francisco jersey, flannel. $400–500

Back of 1961 Willie McCovey jersey, with tail and collar name, flannel. $1800–2200

1969 Shooting star Astros jersey, embroidered logo. $800–1100

1969 Phillies jersey, embroidered, hard to reproduce. $600–$750

Chicago Cubs flannel, #14—Ernie Banks. Wilson, 1969. $1800–2200

Dave McNally flannel jersey, Baltimore Orioles, unusual lettering. $600–700

Chicago Cubs flannel home jersey, 1968. $700–800

Chicago Cubs flannel road jersey, 1967. $600–700

Seattle Pilots one-year jersey, 1969. Restored, \$1000–1300. Most of the Seattle Pilots jerseys that have surfaced have already made their way through the minor leagues and have been restored. An original Pilots jersey that has not been restored is worth \$3000–3500.

Chicago White Sox jersey, Minnie Minoso. \$1,000–\$1,400

Bill Wright Chicago White Sox road jersey. Chenille "Chicago" lettering and felt numbers on the back, with zipper front and 1951 anniversary patch, \$1200–1400. The 50th anniversary patch of the American League on the jersey is valued at \$500–700.

Chicago White Sox road jersey, flannel. $500–600

Atlanta Braves 1970 Hoyt Wilhelm home flannel, Wilson, size 40. This jersey was from "set 4" which is unusual and Wilhelm is a member of the Hall of Fame. $1200–1500

Bill Burbach Yankee home jersey from 1970, flannel, by Spalding. Yankee jerseys are difficult to find because most are recycled through the minor leagues and not made available to collectors. $600–800

Jeff Torborg 1965 Dodger road uniform. Rawlings, size 44, flannel. $700–800

1967 Cincinnati jersey, vest-style. $650–700

The name *under* the numbers is unusual by today's standards.

Red Sox 1967 jersey, flannel.
$400–500

1962 Cleveland Indian flannel.
Size 42, scarce style with a great
deal of wear. $1000

1959 Kansas City Athletics flannel, size 44, elephant is embroidered. The jersey does not have a player's name stitched into it because the A's roster at this point was a "revolving door" with players coming and going constantly. This jersey was found with many others at a flea market and sold by a custodian from the Oakland Coliseum for $7. Over the years Dick Dobbins was able to buy 200 of the jerseys.

Cardinal jersey, flannel, Rawlings, size 42. $600–$700

1969 Reds jersey, Ted Savage. Unusual number on the front. $400–500

1962 Ryne Duren Angels jersey, flannel, restored "Los Angeles", $300–400. If you take a look at the "Los Angeles" lettering, it should become obvious that it has been restored. The letters have been taken from other jerseys to form the word. Compare the "A" and the "G" and note the size differential. These jerseys made long trips through the minor league system and received a great deal of wear.

1971 "one year" style of Clyde Wright with lowercase "a", $500–750

Early Wynn coach's jersey from the 1964 Cleveland Indians, size 50 with stretch material under the armpit, flannel vest-style, by Wilson. $1200–1500

Willie Mays 1963 road jersey, size 44 from Rawlings. $4000–6000

Mays 1963 road jersey from Spalding, size 42, $4000–6000. The two Mays jerseys are from the same season but from different makers (Rawlings and Spalding) and are found in two different sizes.

Flannel Willie McCovey jersey from 1961, size 44, Spalding. It is important to note that there is no consistency in the tagging of jerseys or where the labels can be found. The teams don't have to do things in a lock step so they don't. $2000–3500

1972 Goose Gossage jersey, Chicago White Sox. Size 44 with zipper front, by Wilson. $450–550

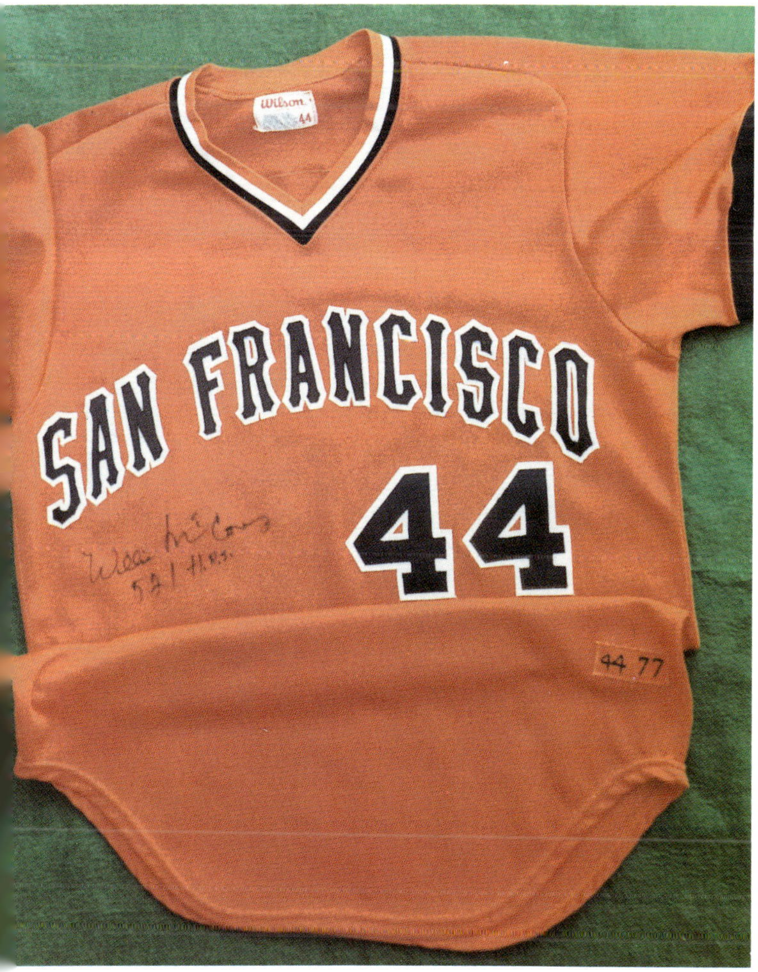

Willie McCovey 1977 Giants jersey, variation with San Francisco on front, Wilson tagging. $1,300–1,500

St. Louis Cardinals knit jersey, Lou Brock. The tail has been cut off and stitched across by Rawlings for Brock. There is no name plate on this jersey. $1,500–2,000

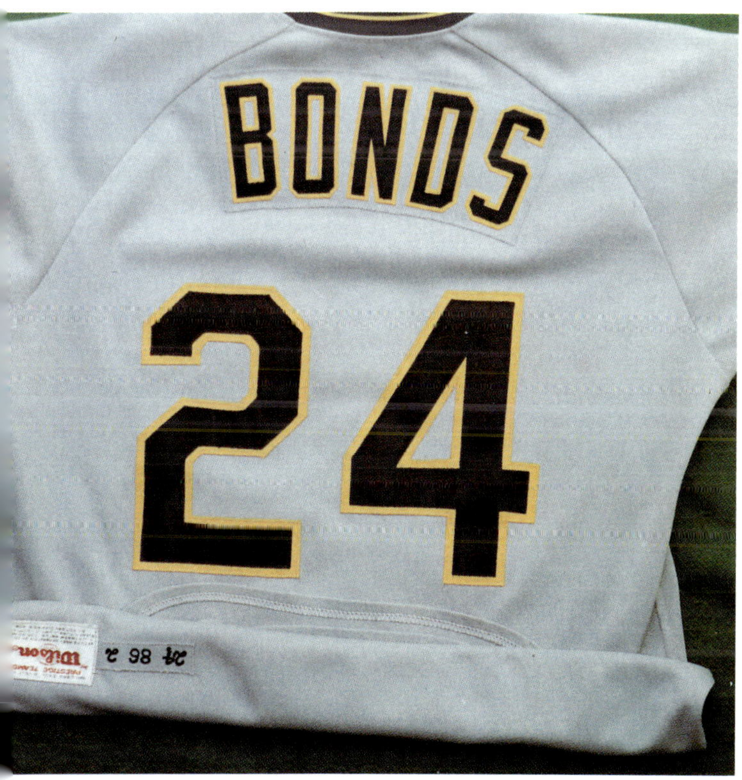

1986 Pittsburgh Pirates jersey with name plate, Barry Bonds, by Wilson. $2,000 plus.

1994 San Francisco Giants jersey of Barry Bonds with Chuck Feeney memorial patch and 125th anniversary of baseball patch, Rawlings. Bonds preferred the Rawlings jersey to the Russell jerseys worn by the Giants so he ordered his own. The Rawlings logo does not appear on the sleeve of the jersey. $1200–1800

Tagging on the Bonds 1994 Rawlings jersey

1983 Rickey Henderson jersey from the Oakland A's, Sand-Knit. Name not on a name plate, very tight jersey. $800–1,000

Von Hayes jersey, Rawlings. Scarce style. $700–775

Rawlings Chicago Cubs jersey, 1990. All-Star patch, size 50 with tapered "T" bottom. $300–350

Chicago Cub jersey, 1990. The All-Star patch makes the jersey unique and can turn a $250 jersey of a common player into a $325–350 jersey.

Red Sox jersey from 1986, wear on the red piping along the button front. $200–250

Button-down Toronto jersey from 1989, $350–450. Toronto jerseys are difficult to find because the team does not sell them in any quantity.

Baltimore jersey of Cal Ripkin with name plate, $3,000–3,500

Hollywood Stars jersey from the Pacific Coast League, 1950. Chenille "Hollywood" on front and number set in a star on the back, possibly only one known. $3,000–4,000

Rawlings Portland Beavers uniform, Pacific Coast League. $300–400

Dallas 1959 jersey from the Texas league, flannel. The initial examination of this minor league jersey would suggest it was worth about $125–150. A minimal amount of research uncovered that it was worn in Dallas by eventual Hall of Famer Willie McCovey and the price escalated considerably.

Maury Wills "fake" jersey from 1965. The Dodger blue fabric is almost impossible to duplicate. This is a bad fake. The tag missing from a superstar jersey is a major hint that there is potentially a serious problem.

"Fake" Don Drysdale jersey, probably a legitimate old jersey that has been seriously manipulated.

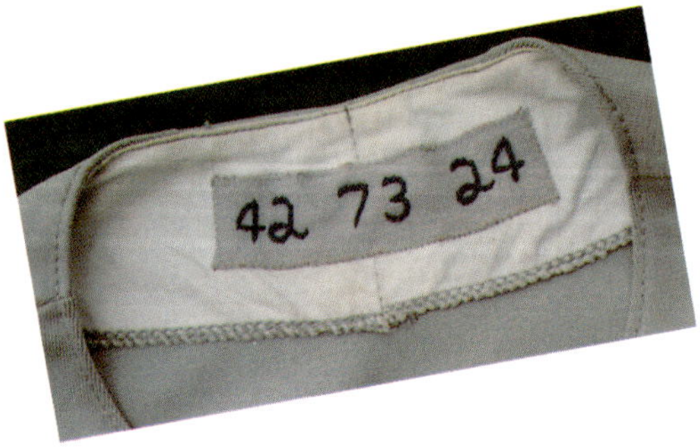

Fake Willie Mays jersey from 1973. Take note of the tagging in the collar. Major league teams use machines to stitch the number, year, and size, and do not use hand stitching. This fake tagging was hand stitched.

Child's baseball glove, c. 1915, "game-worn" condition. $30–40

Minimal padding left little room for error when catching a line drive.

Sporting goods glove of Bert Haas, c. 1940s, $65–75. Haas played from 1937 to 1951 and hit .264 for his career with 22 homeruns.

"Game" glove of Rafael Palmeiro of the Chicago Cubs, 1987, $200–300. This glove was donated to a charity auction by Palmeiro while an outfielder with the Cubs. The glove was made for Palmeiro but was never actually "used" in a game.

Game-used first baseman's glove of Will Clark from the San Francisco Giants. $350–450

Game-worn hat of Shawon Dunston while he was with San Francisco. $35–50

Dunston's autograph and number under the bill of the cap

Carlton Fisk coached for a year at Illinois State University in Normal, Illinois, following his retirement from the White Sox. Fisk has autographed an I.S.U. game hat. $50–65

1950s youth hat from Cy Young League in Ohio. $75–85

Tiger hat signed by Charlie Gehringer shortly before his death in 1993. $100–135

Babe Ruth hat, cereal company premium from the 1930s. $125–200

Newark Eagles hat autographed by Leon Day in Cooperstown in 1994. Day died shortly after being elected to the Hall of Fame in March 1995. $125–150

Giants' "Turn Back the Clock" hat from 1991 game with the Cubs, $45–50. The uniforms and hats were modeled after the 1925 New York Giants.

"Turn Back the Clock" game-used Giants jersey and socks, double-knit version of 1930s uniform. $150–175

"Health" patch on sleeve of "Clock" jersey

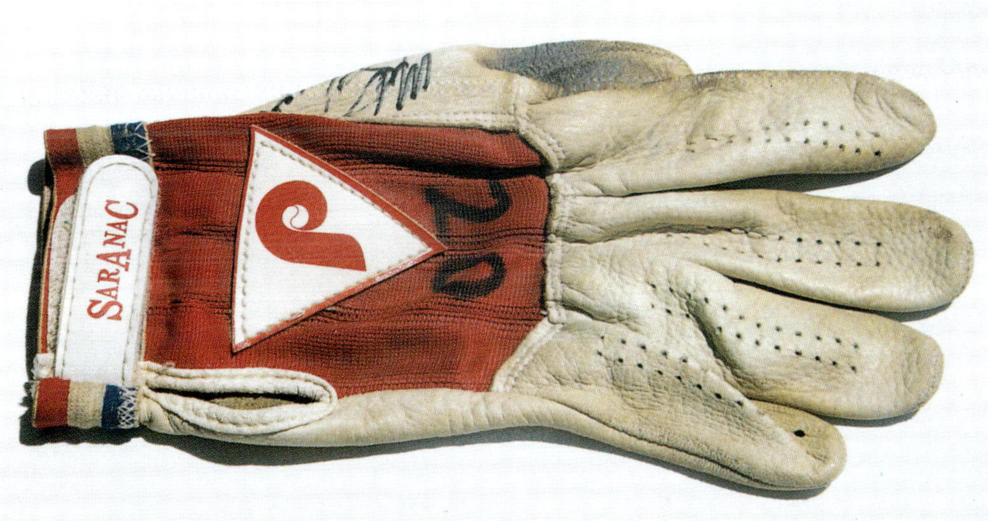

Mike Schmidt batting glove with number and autograph. $125–150

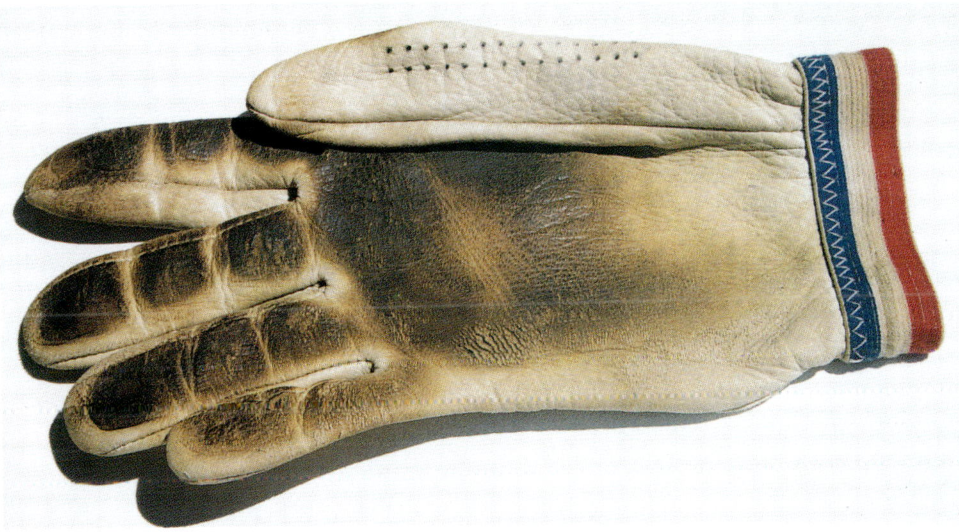

Schmidt autograph and wear on game-used batting glove.

Game-used batting glove of Montreal catcher Gary Carter. $100–125

Atlanta Braves batting helmet of Claudell Washington, c. 1986. $75–100

A batting helmet of a player of the stature of Washington would rarely be faked or reproduced because of its lack of interest from collectors. It would be just as easy to fake a Dale Murphy and get two or three times the money.

Game-worn spikes of Mike Schmidt, c. 1984. $400–500

Schmidt autographed both shoes along the Nike logo with a blue Sharpie, which is beginning to fade.

Game-worn spikes of Shawon Dunston while he was with San Francisco, $75–100. Dunston is a classic example of a player whose equipment peaked fairly quickly in value early in his career and gradually diminished as he moved from team to team.

Game-used Spot-bilt spikes of George Brett. $400–500

Autographed locker door from the Peoria Chiefs used by Greg Maddux while pitching for Peoria in the Midwest League. $200–250

The autographed door was sold by the Peoria Chiefs following a clubhouse remodeling.

Limited edition Hall of Fame bat that commemorates the 1936 induction, 15 autographs, $700–1000. These bats have been issued periodically since 1983. Each bat lists the players inducted in a given year.

1936 induction bat signed by Mantle.

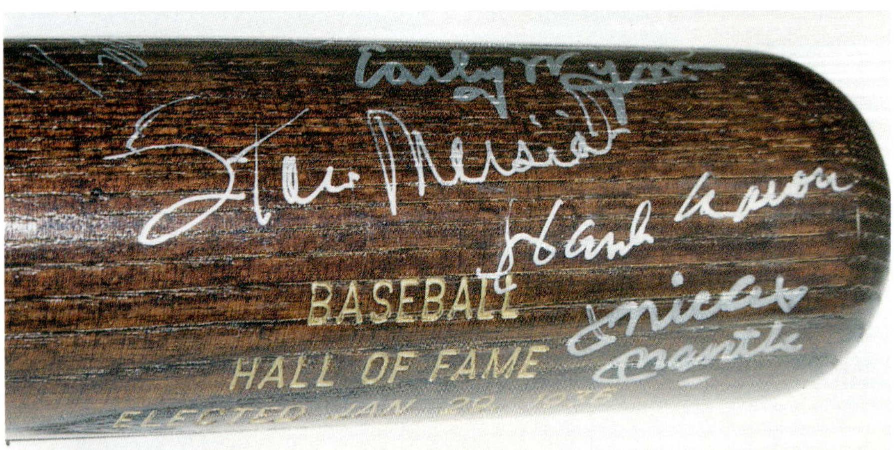

Musial, Aaron, and Mantle on the 1936 bat.

1939 Hall of Fame induction bat with impressed signatures of Gehrig, Sisler, and Eddie Collins.

1981 induction bat autographed by Johnny Mize and Bob Gibson. $325–400

1983 induction bat autographed by Brooks Robinson. $375–450

George Kell's autograph on the 1983 induction bat.

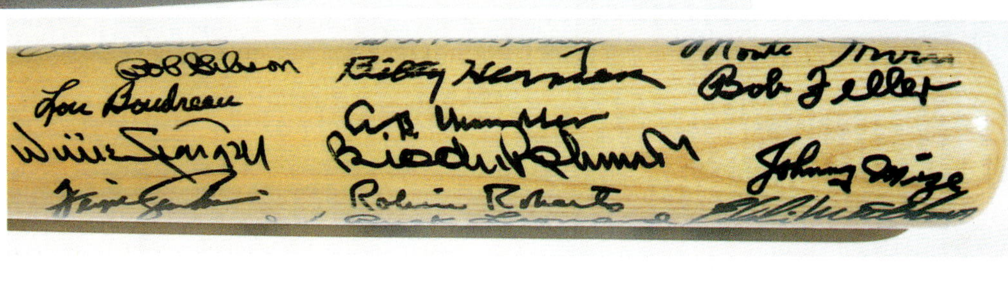

Cooperstown Bat Company bat autographed by 24 members of the Hall of Fame in Cooperstown in 1983. $450–600

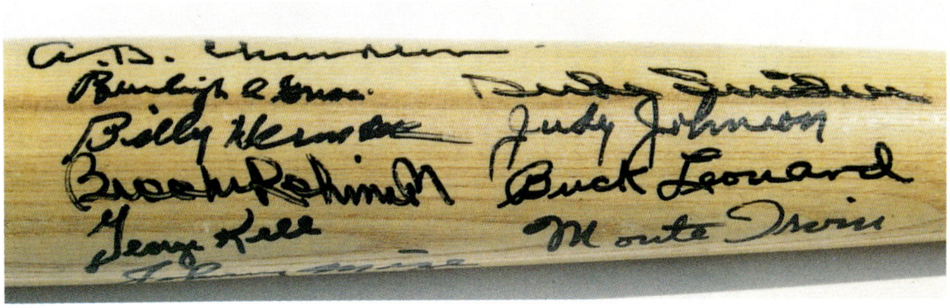

Bat autographed in Cooperstown in 1983 by 21 members of the Hall of Fame, $400–500. There is a pre-stroke signature of Buck Leonard and a rare autograph of Burleigh Grimes (d. 1985) on the bat.

Game bat of Robin Yount of the Brewers, autographed with a black Sharpie. $200–250

Yount's autograph on his game bat

Game-used bat of John Kruk from the Phillies, c. 1992. $150–165

Kruk's autograph in black Sharpie

Kruk's #29 on the underside of the knob so it can easily be pulled from the bat rack.

Game-used Mike Lansing bat of the Expo's, c. 1997. $65–75

Carlton Fisk's game bat, autographed with a black Sharpie. $300–375

Lansing's #3 in black Sharpie on the bat.

Game-used Williams bat, uncracked, c. 1975. $100–125. Unfortunately, this bat was used by "No Neck" Williams rather than Ted Williams. The difference in value is probably $5000–6000.

Larry Walker's game-used cracked bat from Montreal. $75–100

Game-used Yankee team bat, uncracked. $50–65

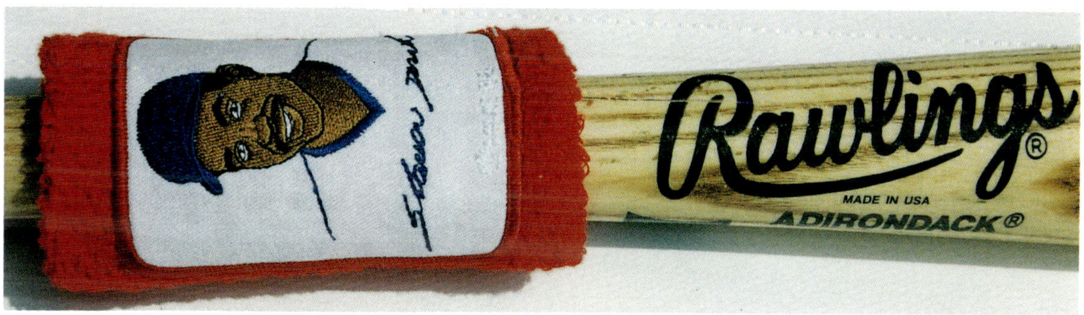

Game wrist band of Shawon Dunston with the Cubs. $15–$20

Bat autographed by Joe Sewell, Hall of Fame shortstop, in 1988. Mr. Sewell died in 1990. $250–275

Game-used bat by Shawon Dunston during his brief first stay with San Francisco. $65–75

Ozzie Smith game-used bat from the Cardinals. $200–250

#1 in black Sharpie on knob of Smith bat

Uncracked game-used Fred Lynn bat. $100–125

Lynn's autograph on his bat

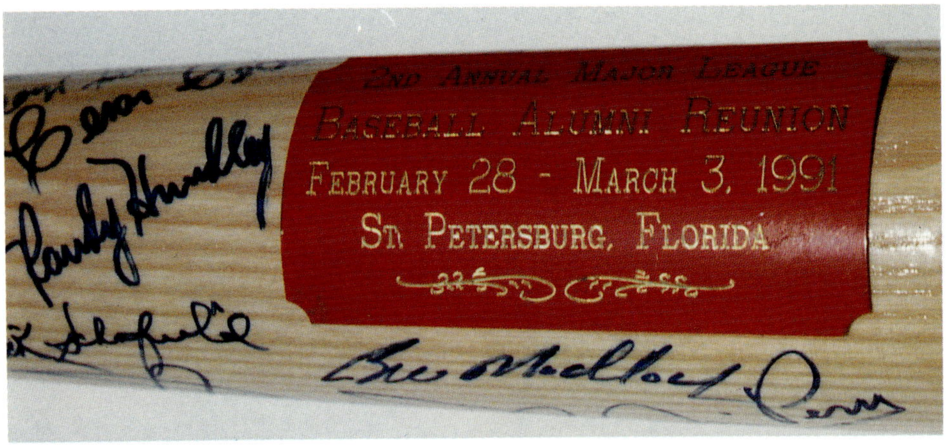

Commemorative bat autographed at the Baseball Alumni Reunion in St. Petersburg, Florida in 1991. $200–275

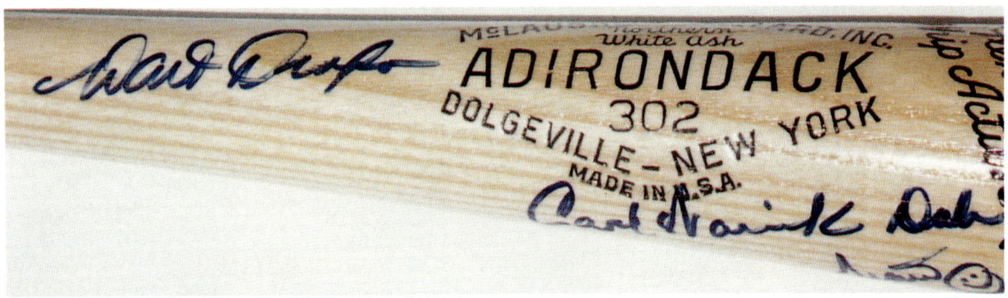

Signatures of Dropo and Carl Warwick on the Adirondack bat

Signatures of Hall of Famers Brooks Robinson, Monte Irvin and Bob Feller

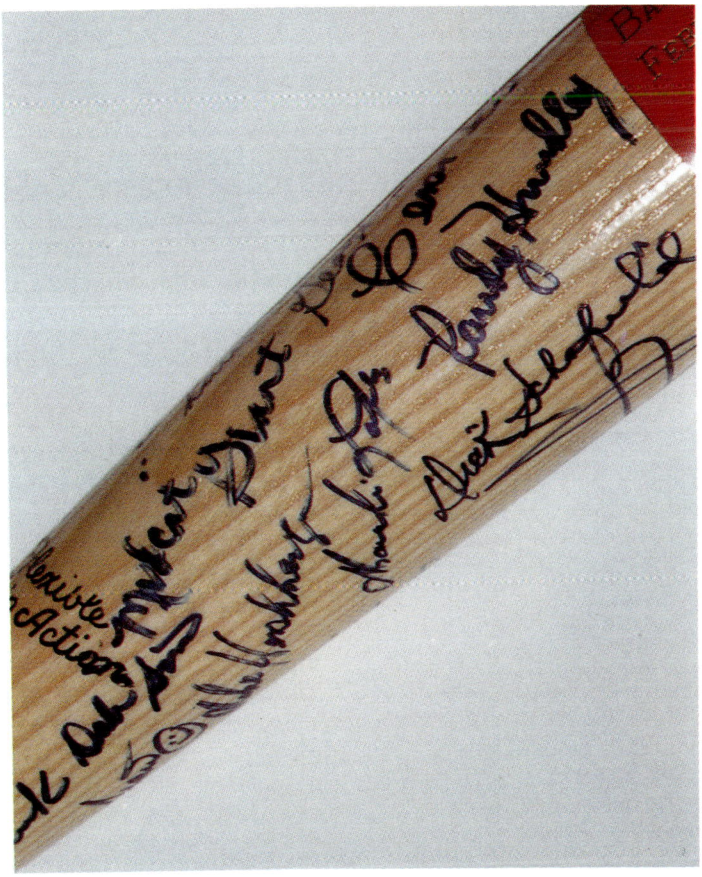

Signatures of Dick Scofield, Randy Hundley, and Mudcat Grant

Game-used bat of former Kansas City slugger Steve Balboni. $50–65

1991 "First Five" set of bats produced by the Cooperstown Bat Company and the Hall of Fame to honor Ruth, Mathewson, Cobb, Wagner, and Walter Johnson. The bats are modeled after the "decal" bats of the 1910–1915 period. $1500 (sct of five)

Hall of Fame decal on the Ruth bat

The five bats specific in this set are each numbered 127 out of a set of 500 total

Ty Cobb "First Five"decal bat

Little League Ralph Kiner bat c. 1953, "decal" on barrel. $25–40

Mike Schmidt autographed commemorative bat honoring his 1981 MVP award. $200–250

Game-used Mike Schmidt bat. Autographed, c. early 1980s, cracked. $500–650

Game-used Moises Alou bat from Montreal, c. 1995. $75–90

Game-used Daryl Strawberry bat from San Francisco, autographed. $135–150

Babe Ruth model bat offered in limited numbers by J. Peterman Company in early 1990s. Autographed by four members of the 500 home run club.$300–400

Autograph of Willie McCovey on the Ruth bat

Ted Williams signature on the Ruth bat

Uncracked game-used bat of former Montreal second baseman Jim Cox. $25–35

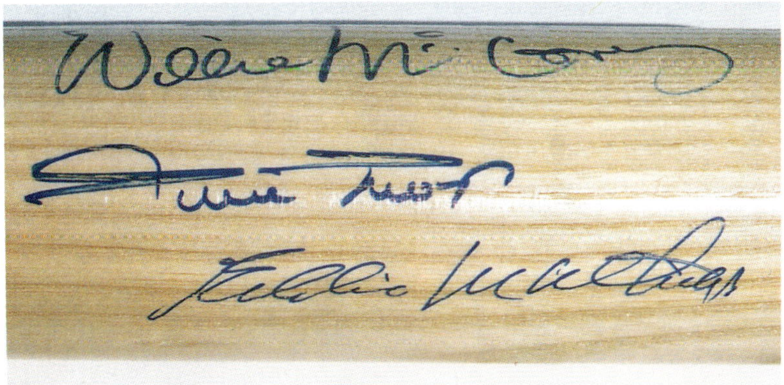

Autographs of Mathews, Mays, McCovey on the Ruth bat

Rare Louisville Slugger bat rack c. 1940s from a sporting goods store. $1000–1400

Top left: Bat chair made from 23 game-used major league bats by Fairbury, Illinois artisan Marty Travis. $1000–1200

Bottom: Back of the bat chair.

Top right: Seat of the chair showing the bats of Sid Fernandez, Sherman Obando, Julio Cruz, Jeff King, Derrick May & Ron Hassey.

Chapter 3

Autographs

Collectors who are on a mission to acquire an example of the autograph from every member of the Hall of Fame will face an extremely difficult task that is compounded by the fact that at least seven of the members died prior to 1900. Attempting to secure signatures from individuals who have been dead for more than a century is going to be a serious challenge. Autographed photographs or balls from these gentlemen do not exist. At best a "cut" from a letter, receipt, check, or legal document is the most promising possibility.

The problem, once you locate one of these signatures, is to authenticate it before you spend the $1,500 to $3,000 it's going to cost to own it. We once had an opportunity to examine the will of Charles Radbourn at the McLean County clerk's office in Bloomington, Illinois. Radbourn died in 1897. The highlight of his career was winning 59 or 60 games (baseball scholars differ on the number) during the 1884 season with the Providence Grays in the National League.

Radbourn's signature on the will is unlike any other example we have seen for sale or illustrated in several books about autographs. The signature on the will is "right" because it was witnessed by four of his contemporaries and eventually was probated after his demise. If you use the signature in the will as your benchmark, you might not find another legitimate Radbourn autograph.

The gentlemen listed below would certainly be among the most difficult Hall of Fame autographs to add to a collection. As noted above when their signatures are found, they tend to be "cuts" rather than a full document, letter, or check.

- "Rube" Foster
- Ed Delahanty
- William Hulbert
- George Davis
- "Old Hoss" Radbourn
- Mickey Welsh
- Addie Joss
- Roger Connor
- Vic Willis
- John Clarkson
- Ned Hanlon
- Jake Beckley
- Mike Kelly
- Bullet Joe Rogan
- Candy Cummings

Historical Perspective

On June 12, 1939 William Gauger, Jr. of Philadelphia, Pennsylvania was in Cooperstown, New York for the opening of the Hall of Fame. Gauger purchased an assortment of first day covers and cachets that he had postmarked. He probably saw U.S. Postmaster James Farley who also was in Cooperstown that day for the unveiling of the baseball centennial stamp.

After he arrived back in Philadelphia, he sent the first day covers to the eleven Hall of Fame members who attended the ceremonies. These included Eddie Collins, Babe Ruth, Connie Mack, Cy Young, Honus Wagner, Grover Alexander, Tris Speaker, Nap Lajoie, George Sisler, Walter Johnson, and Ty Cobb. All responded positively to Gauger's requests for their autographs.

He also enclosed a single first day cover that eventually was signed by all eleven. In addition to the players, Gauger mailed a first day cover to league presidents, Frick and Harridge, and commissioner Landis for their signatures.

In a relatively short period he was able to secure the autographs of eleven of baseball's immortals for a couple of 3¢ stamps and a self-addressed envelope. If you wrote to eleven of baseball's superstars today, you would get absolutely nothing back except several of the envelopes marked "refused."

Gauger wrote to Tris Speaker asking about the address of Cy Young. Young won 511 games during his major league career. Speaker wrote back to Gauger and informed him that Young was working as a sergeant-at-arms at the state capital in Columbus, Ohio. Gauger then contacted Young and he graciously signed the items sent to him.

He also wrote to Babe Ruth requesting the address of Grover Cleveland Alexander. Ruth responded that "I have no idea where of the players live" and signed "Babe."

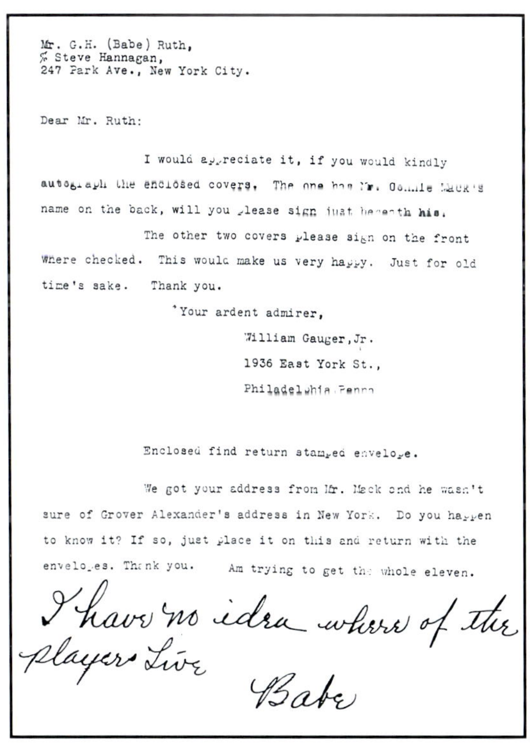
Mr. G.H. (Babe) Ruth,
% Steve Hannagan,
247 Park Ave., New York City.

Dear Mr. Ruth:

I would appreciate it, if you would kindly autograph the enclosed covers. The one has Mr. Connie Mack's name on the back, will you please sign just beneath his.

The other two covers please sign on the front where checked. This would make us very happy. Just for old time's sake. Thank you.

Your ardent admirer,
William Gauger, Jr.
1936 East York St.,
Philadelphia, Penna.

Enclosed find return stamped envelope.

We got your address from Mr. Mack and he wasn't sure of Grover Alexander's address in New York. Do you happen to know it? If so, just place it on this and return with the envelopes. Thank you. Am trying to get the whole eleven.

I have no idea where of the players Live
Babe

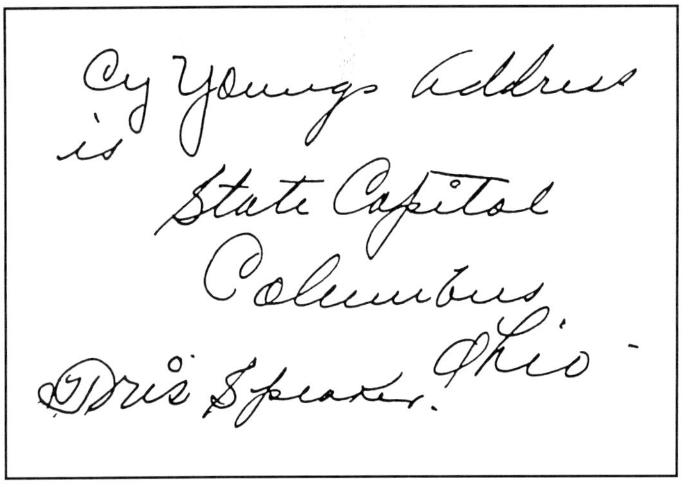
Cy Youngs Address
is
State Capitol
Columbus
Ohio
Tris Speaker

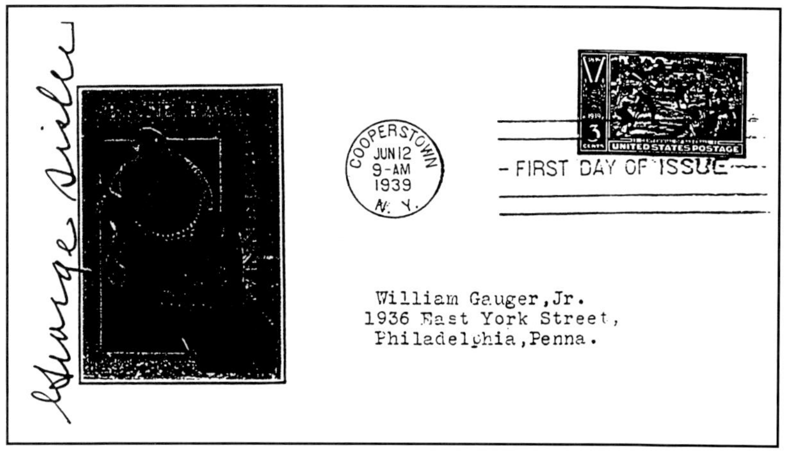
George Sisler
COOPERSTOWN
JUN 12
9-AM
1939
N.Y.
3 CENTS UNITED STATES POSTAGE
- FIRST DAY OF ISSUE -
William Gauger, Jr.
1936 East York Street,
Philadelphia, Penna.

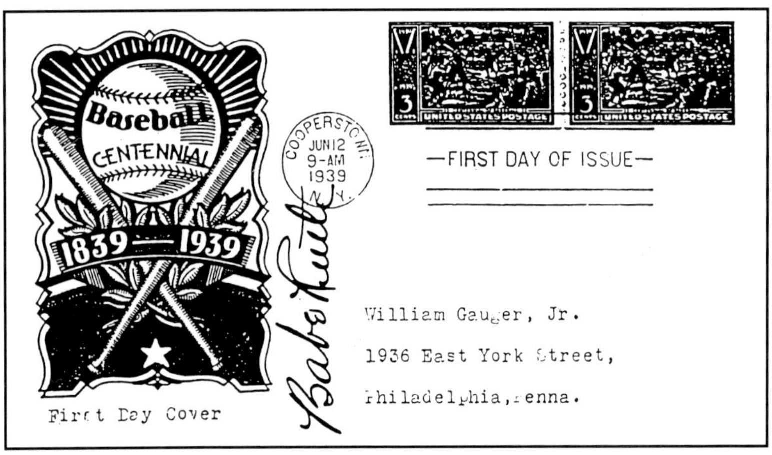
Baseball
CENTENNIAL
1839 — 1939
First Day Cover
Babe Ruth
COOPERSTOWN N.Y.
JUN 12
9-AM
1939
3 CENTS UNITED STATES POSTAGE
—FIRST DAY OF ISSUE—
William Gauger, Jr.
1936 East York Street,
Philadelphia, Penna.

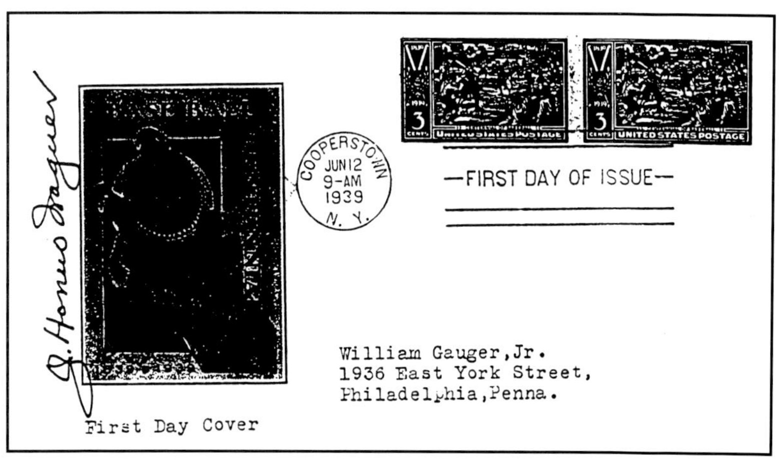
J. Honus Wagner
COOPERSTOWN
JUN 12
9-AM
1939
N.Y.
3 CENTS UNITED STATES POSTAGE
—FIRST DAY OF ISSUE—
William Gauger, Jr.
1936 East York Street,
Philadelphia, Penna.
First Day Cover

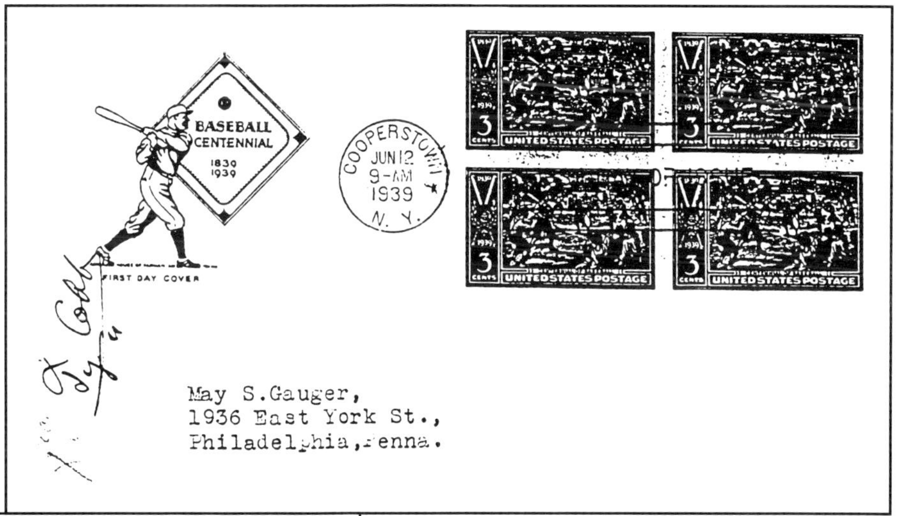
BASEBALL CENTENNIAL
1839 1939
FIRST DAY COVER
COOPERSTOWN JUN 12 9-AM 1939 N. Y.
3 CENTS UNITED STATES POSTAGE
May S.Gauger,
1936 East York St.,
Philadelphia,Penna.

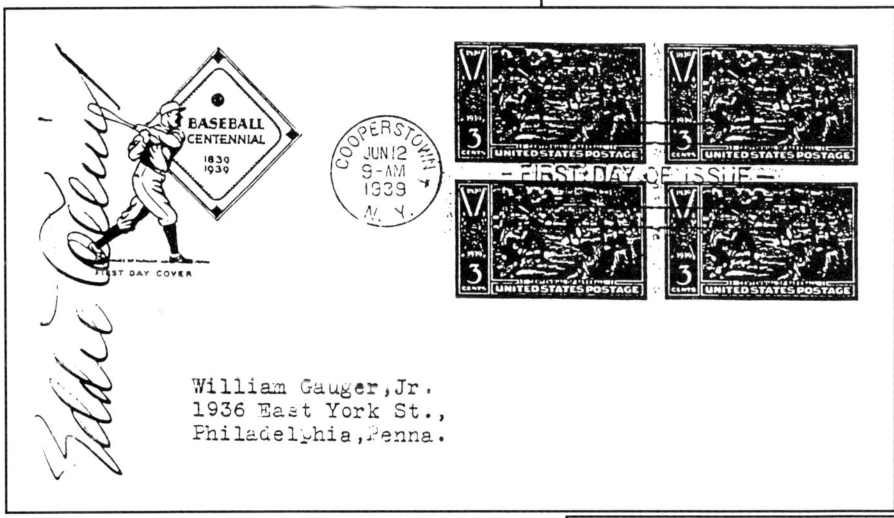
BASEBALL CENTENNIAL
1839 1939
FIRST DAY COVER
COOPERSTOWN JUN 12 9-AM 1939 N. Y.
3 CENTS UNITED STATES POSTAGE
FIRST DAY OF ISSUE
William Gauger,Jr.
1936 East York St.,
Philadelphia,Penna.

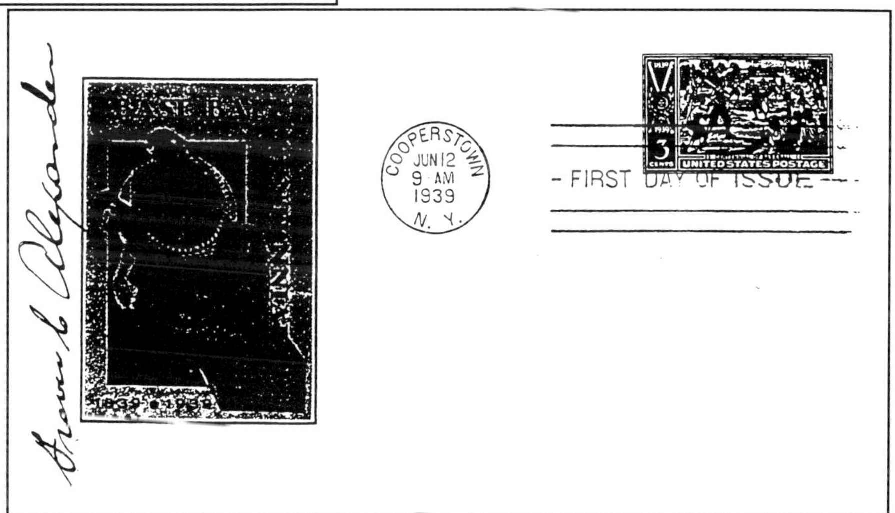
COOPERSTOWN JUN 12 9 AM 1939 N. Y.
3 UNITED STATES POSTAGE
FIRST DAY OF ISSUE

BASEBALL
1839 • 1939
COOPERSTOWN JUN 12 9-AM 1939 N. Y.
3 UNITED STATES POSTAGE
FIRST DAY OF ISSUE
William Gauger,Jr.
1936 E.York St.,
Philadelphia,Pa.

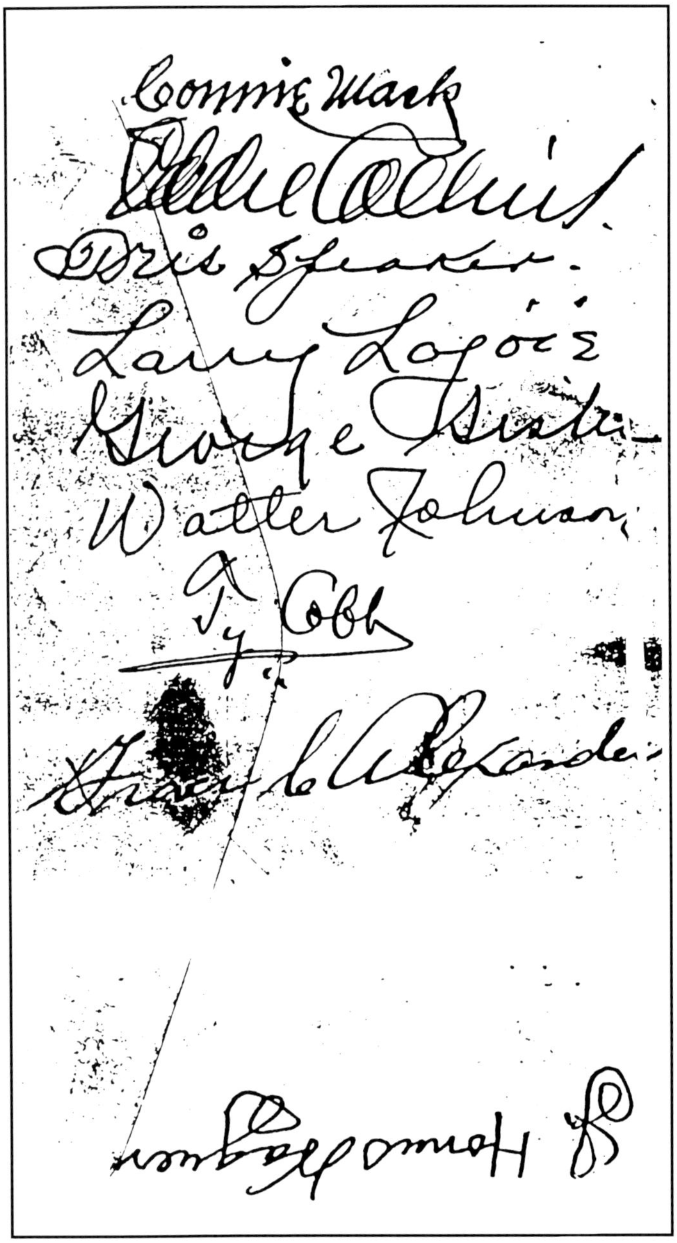

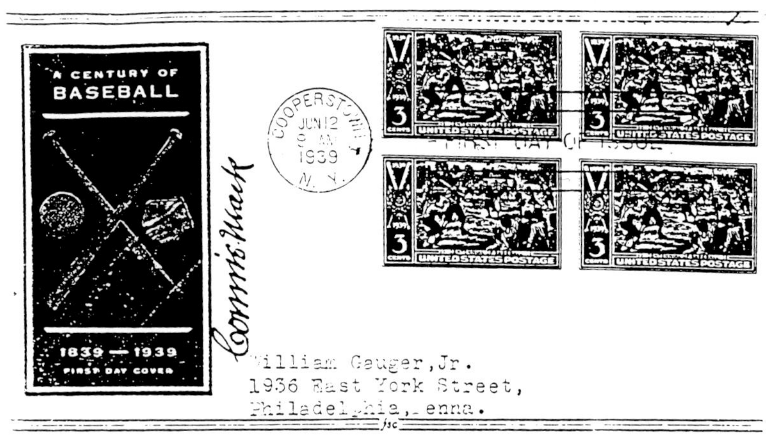

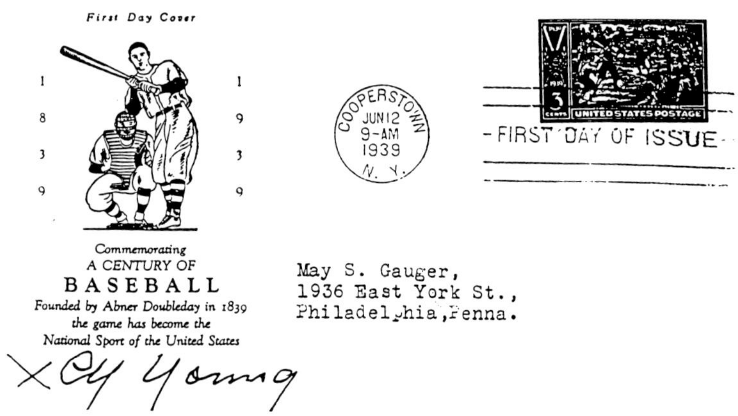

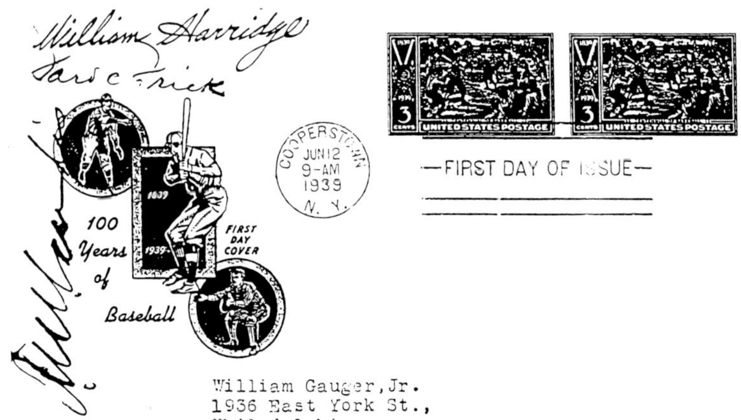

Contemporary Hall of Fame Autograph Opportunities

The individuals listed below all took part in autograph sessions at baseball card shows around the country, private signings, or public signings in Cooperstown after 1980. Their autographs should not be too difficult to obtain because most have made numerous appearances.

Keep in mind that baseball card shows with autograph guests are largely a product of the 1980s. As the demand for cards diminished in the 1990s, the number of shows also gradually declined. Current baseball stars and superstars make so much money that setting aside three hours of their lives to deal with the general public at a show is not appealing to many.

Pitchers
Jim Bunning
Steve Carlton
Don Drysdale*
Bob Feller
Rollie Fingers
Whitey Ford
Bob Gibson
Lefty Gomez*
Burleigh Grimes*
Catfish Hunter
Ferguson Jenkins
Sandy Koufax
Bob Lemon
Juan Marichal
Hal Newhouser
Phil Niekro
Jim Palmer
Gaylord Perry
Robin Roberts
Tom Seaver

Warren Spahn
Don Sutton
Early Wynn
Hoyt Wilhelm

Catchers
Johnny Bench
Yogi Berra
Bill Dickey*
Rick Ferrell*

First Basemen
Harmon Killebrew
Willie McCovey
Johnny Mize*
Bill Terry*

Second Basemen
Rod Carew
Bobby Doerr
Charlie Gehringer*
Billy Herman*
Joe Morgan
Red Schoendienst

Third Basemen
George Kell
Eddie Mathews
Brooks Robinson

Mike Schmidt

Shortstops
Luis Aparicio
Luke Appling*
Ernie Banks
Lou Boudreau
Pee Wee Reese
Phil Rizzuto
Joe Sewell*

Centerfielders
Richie Ashburn*
Joe DiMaggio
Larry Doby
Mickey Mantle*
Willie Mays
Duke Snider

Rightfielders
Hank Aaron
Reggie Jackson
Al Kaline
Frank Robinson
Enos Slaughter

Leftfielders
Lou Brock
Ralph Kiner

Stan Musial
Willie Stargell
Billy Williams
Ted Williams
Carl Yastrzemski

Managers
Leo Durocher*
Tommy Lasorda
Al Lopez
Earl Weaver

Umpires
Al Barlick*
Jocko Conlan*

Executives
Happy Chandler*

Negro Leagues
Ray Dandridge*
Leon Day*
Monte Irvin
Judy Johnson*
Buck Leonard*

*Deceased

Labor Day 1988

On Labor Day weekend 1988, twenty major league players signed autographs at a show in California. Ten years later it appears that we all probably should have been there with our bats, pictures, and balls in hand.

When is the next time Mark McGwire is going to be signing your baseball or bat for $8 ($7 if the ticket is ordered in advance)? Willie Mays can be as sullen and unpleasant as he wants if he will sign our bat for $9 ($8 if ordered in advance).

We would even think about buying all our tickets in advance to have Musial, Mays, Aaron, Marichal, Gibson, Snider, Stargell, Brock, Killebrew, Brooks Robinson, Perry, Feller, and Fingers on our Hall of Fame bat for a total of $65.

At those prices we might even have two bats signed.

ALL-AMERICAN SUPERSTAR LINE-UP:

In Person Autographs			Mail Order Autographs			
Players Appearing	Day	Autograph Ticket	Autographed Official Ball	Autographed 8x10 Color Photo	Autographed Official Bat	Your Flat Item Autographed
Willie MAYS	Mon.	$9.00	$16.00	$11.00	$69.00	$10.00
Hank AARON	Sat./Sun.	8.00	15.00	10.00	69.00	9.00
Jose CANSECO	Sat.	8.00	15.00	10.00	69.00	9.00
Mark McGWIRE	Sat.	8.00	15.00	10.00	69.00	9.00
Stan MUSIAL	Fri./Sat.	8.00	15.00	10.00	69.00	9.00
Juan MARICHAL	Fri.	6.00	12.00	8.00	—	7.00
Bob GIBSON	Mon.	6.00	12.00	8.00	—	7.00
Duke SNIDER	Sat.	6.00	12.00	8.00	49.00	7.00
Willie STARGELL	Mon.	6.00	12.00	8.00	49.00	7.00
Lou BROCK	Fri.	6.00	12.00	8.00	49.00	7.00
Harmon KILLEBREW	Sun.	5.00	11.00	7.00	49.00	6.00
Brooks ROBINSON	Sat.	5.00	11.00	7.00	49.00	6.00
Orlando CEPEDA	Sun./Mon.	5.00	11.00	7.00	49.00	6.00
Gaylord PERRY	Sun.	5.00	11.00	7.00	—	6.00
Bob FELLER	4 days	4.00	10.00	6.00	—	5.00
Rollie FINGERS	Fri.	4.00	10.00	6.00	—	5.00
Don LARSEN	Sun.	4.00	10.00	6.00	—	5.00
Denny McLAIN	Mon.	4.00	10.00	6.00	—	5.00
Bobby THOMSON	Fri.	4.00	10.00	6.00	—	5.00
Joe RUDI	Fri.	4.00	10.00	6.00	—	5.00

Purchase All-American Convention advance autograph and admission tickets at our upcoming shows, or by mail. Deduct $1.00 off listed prices on each autograph and admission ticket by ordering early!

Investment Potential of Hall of Fame Autographs

We have constructed two lists of Hall of Fame members who signed autographs after 1980 at shows, public signings, or private signings. List A contains 12 we feel will have the most long term investment potential for baseballs they have single-signed. List B contains the names of 12 Hall of Fame members who also signed after 1980 with the least long term investment potential.

Ted Williams and Joe DiMaggio are on the list for their long term investment potential. Both have signed several thousands of items over the years. Many people initially purchased more of their signatures than they normally would considering the "baseball immortal" status of both men and the thought of huge returns on their investment. It will eventually come, but it may be several decades away because of the vast amount of material that has been signed by both men. In our opinion, the best DiMaggio and Williams investment for the least amount of dollars are autographed yellow Hall of Fame plaques (postcards).

List A: Most Potential
Jocko Conlan (d. 1989)
Lefty Gomez (d. 1989)
Bill Dickey (d. 1993)
Burleigh Grimes (d. 1985)
Joe Sewell (d. 1990)
Bill Terry (d. 1989)
Leon Day (d. 1995)
Judy Johnson (d. 1989)
Leo Durocher (d. 1991)
Ted Williams
Joe DiMaggio
Al Lopez
Sandy Koufax

List B: Least Potential
Monte Irvin
Lou Boudreau
Luis Aparicio
George Kell
Red Schoendienst
Hoyt Wilhelm
Bob Feller
Bob Lemon
Warren Spahn
Enos Slaughter
Ferguson Jenkins
Robin Roberts

Hall of Fame Membership Potential

Contemporary Players, Managers, & Executives

It is probably a wise investment to secure the autograph of potential Hall of Famers prior to their election. Once a player is inducted into the Hall of Fame, the cost of his autograph rises dramatically and his accessibility diminishes.

As we noted, almost every living player elected to the Hall of Fame since 1980 has done autograph sessions at shows or in Cooperstown during the Induction Weekend. Many have also done private signings. The only reasons a player is not on the autograph circuit are due to disinterest or failing health.

To be elected to the Hall of Fame, a player must have been active at some time during the period beginning 20 years before and ending five years prior to his election. He must have played a minimum of ten seasons in the major leagues. Players not elected during this eligibility period can be considered by the Veterans Committee after they meet its requirements.

* will be in the Hall of Fame
** could be in the Hall of Fame

*** way too soon to tell, but the early returns are positive

zero stars: will receive a significant number of votes, but will probably fall short of election

Players
Ken Griffey, Jr. *
Barry Larkin **
Pedro Martinez ***
Alex Rodriguez ***
Randy Johnson **
Jeff Bagwell
Juan Gonzalez **
Roger Clemens *
Barry Bonds *
Frank Thomas *
Mariano Rivera
Craig Biggio
Nomar Garciaparra ***
Andy Pettitte ***
Mark McGwire *
Roberto Alomar **
Dennis Eckersley *
Sammy Sosa***
Matt Williams
Derek Jeter ***
Edgar Martinez
Andres Galarraga
Ivan Rodriguez *
Curt Schilling
Sammy Sosa
Chuck Knoblauch
Tom Glavine
Ben Grieve ***
Albert Belle
Scott Rolen ***
Fred McGriff
Mo Vaughn **
Gregg Maddux *
Rickey Henderson*
Cal Ripkin Jr. *
Tony Gwynn *
Paul Molitor *
Mike Piazza *
Joe Carter **
Larry Walker
Wade Boggs *
Bernie Williams
Chipper Jones ***
Charles Johnson
Vladimir Guerrero

Managers
Bobby Cox *
Tony LaRussa **
Jim Leyland **
Joe Torre**

Executive
Leonard Coleman ***

Selected Recently Retired Players

First year of eligibility for the Hall of Fame:

2000: Rich Gossage, Jack Morris, Jeff Reardon
2001: Don Mattingly, Kirby Puckett, Dave Winfield, Lou Whitaker, Dave Stewart
2002: Andre Dawson, Ozzie Smith, Alan Trammal

Will Be Elected
Puckett
Winfield
Smith

Probably Will Be Elected At Some Point
Dawson
Murphy

Might Be Elected
Mattingly
Morris
Gossage

Two Executives, Ten Players, and One Manager Who Will Make the Hall of Fame

The list that follows includes 13 individuals who are going to be elected to the Hall of Fame. It may not be next year or in 20 years but they will be inducted. With the exception of Thurman Munson, Gil Hodges, Joe Gordon, and Ken Boyer their autographs are still plentiful and reasonably priced. We would suggest that you purchase any single-signed baseballs in your price range of these gentlemen when you come upon them. They are seriously underpriced today when compared with what they are going to be when their names are added to the roster of the Hall of Fame. Trust us, it is not a question of "if," it is a question of "when."

Players
Bert Blyleven: 287 wins
Ken Boyer*: 282 home runs and 5 gold gloves at third base
Joe Gordon*: 253 home runs at second base
Tommy John: 288 victories
Gil Hodges*: Brooklyn slugger and Met manager
Jim Kaat: 286 wins and 16 gold gloves
Thurman Munson*: Yankee catcher whose career was cut short by his premature death in a plane crash.
Ron Santo: One of the greatest third basemen of all-time
Ted Simmons: Considered by many to be among the two or three best hitting catchers of all time.
Cecil Travis: Hit .359 with 218 hits in 1941 before losing three seasons to World War II. Hit .314 at shortstop for Washington over his career.

Manager
Billy Martin*: Won 5 divisional titles, 2 pennants, 1 World Series.

Executives
Charles O. Finley*: Controversial innovator who led his team to World Championships in Oakland
Bowie Kuhn: Commissioner who battled Finley and consistently made the hard decisions based on what he thought was best for baseball.

*Deceased

Notes on Collecting Baseball Autographs

1. If you attend an autograph-card show, make every effort to buy your autograph tickets in advance.
2. Be aware of what the autograph guest will and will not sign. Some players will not autograph certain cards, pictures, books, or bats. Over the years, Joe DiMaggio has been especially sensitive about what he signs. The specific restrictions are usually spelled out in advertisements prior to the show.
3. There are usually different fees for different items that are going to be autographed. Bats and uniforms will be considerably more expensive to have autographed than balls or "flats". The size of the "flats" often dictates the signing fee.
4. Take the pen you want the guest to use to sign your items as "back up" even though there will be a plentiful supply on the signing table. At some point in your collecting career you will be standing in front of the autograph guest and he will not have the correct pen for you and you will have six seconds to find an alternative. It could be as simple as substituting a black Sharpie for a blue one on a football or baseball bat.
5. Assume the following will happen at the card show:
   a. The autograph guest will be late.
   b. The show promoter will lean more to mass confusion rather than organization.
   c. The signing rules will be changed three or four times.
   d. When your hero signs your item, he won't look up.
   e. When you arrive at the show, shop around for the best price on 8 x 10 photographs of the guest. Many of the dealers will offer the same picture at different prices.
   f. American and National League baseballs often are more expensive at the show than in other venues. Bring your own baseballs. If you get stuck at the show without a ball, shop around for the best price.
6. The dealers' prices at the show usually have some built-in flexibility. Do not hesitate to ask the following questions:
   a. What's the best you can do on that?
   b. What's your best price?
   c. How much if I buy both?

Notes on Fountain Pens, Ballpoint Pens, and Felt Tip Pens

The fountain pen is largely a product of the mid-1880s. By the mid-1890s it was affordable, in common use, and readily available at the neighborhood drug store or stationary store.

The ballpoint pen was made available to the public after World War II (mid-1940s) and could be easily found by the early 1950s. Babe Ruth died on August 16, 1948 and *could* have signed some autographs with a ballpoint but the vast majority of Ruth signatures were executed with a fountain pen.

The time frame between Ruth's demise and the rise of the ballpoint pen is so brief that Ruth autographs in ballpoint should be closely examined before being purchased. The Ruth personal checks that we have seen offered for sale from the 1946–48 period of his life are still in fountain pen.

The felt tip pen first became available in the mid 1960s and was inexpensively found everywhere by the early 1970s.

Notes on Paint Pens, the "Sharpie", and the Bic Ballpoint

1. Paint pens can be difficult to use and a concern if the silver or gold gets on clothes. Players often avoid the paint pen because of its potential for problems.
2. The flow of gold or silver "paint" from the pen can sometimes be inconsistent and destroy the quality of the signature. The paint can also chip or flake away over time. Nobody knows for sure how long the paint pen signature will last.
3. There are some basic rules of use for the "Sharpie":
   a. Avoid any color but blue or black.
   b. Blue can gradually turn purple on baseball bats.
   c. Black on paper or baseballs tends to pick up a yellow "shadow" over time.
   d. Blue on baseballs tend to "bleed" (expand) and eventually fade.
4. The blue ink Bic ballpoint is the pen of choice for baseballs; avoid any color other than blue.
5. Some collectors recommend using a ballpoint pen on cards and photographs that date from the 1950s–1960s because the "Sharpie" didn't exist during that period. We have never been impressed with the quality of the signature made by the ballpoint on photographs and cards, even though it is probably historically accurate.
6. **Exceptions**–When the article to be signed is too dark for a black or blue "Sharpie", the silver or gold paint pen is a viable alternative. Listed below are examples of some of the items where the paint pen may be warranted:

1. Black or brown baseball bats
2. Helmets that are dark or black
3. Especially dark photographs (black & white or color)
4. Dark or black caps
5. Black shoes

Item	Silver or Gold Paint Pen	Blue Sharpie	Black Sharpie	Bic Blue Ballpoint Pen
Baseball Bat			✍	
Baseball				✍
Football	✍		✍	
Basketball	✍		✍	
Gold HOF Plaque		✍		
3 x 5 Card		✍		✍
B & W Photo		✍		
Color Photo		✍		
Hockey puck	✍			
Football or Baseball Helmet		✍	✍	
Baseball Cap		✍	✍	
Jersey		✍	✍	
Leather Shoes			✍	
Baseball Card		✍		

Autograph Values

The autographed items evaluated below are assumed to be in at least "very good" to "excellent" condition. The signatures are bold and legible. We have selected this cross-section of baseball legends to provide some general insight into autograph prices and what is still available to collectors.

	Single-Signed Baseball	Picture	"Cut"	HOF Gold Plaque
Grover Cleveland Alexander	$3,000	$1,200	$300	~
Ty Cobb	$2,500	$900	$275	~
Hugh Duffy	$2,000	$650	$275	~
Jimmie Foxx	$1,800	$750	$200	$1,200
Lou Gehrig	$4,000	$2,000	$700	~
Hank Greenberg	$350	$125	$35	$100
Rogers Hornsby	$1,500	$500	$200	~
Reggie Jackson	$65	$45	$25	$35
Judy Johnson	$250	$35	$15	$45
George Kelly	$135	$50	$15	$45
Tony Lazzeri	$1,800	$400	$175	~
Al Lopez	$100	$55	$20	$50
Roger Maris	$400	$250	$95	~
Stan Musial	$65	$45	$20	$35
Charles Nichols	$3,200	$800	$400	~
Charles Radbourn	~	~	$2,200	~
Jackie Robinson	$1,850	$1,000	$350	$1,000
Babe Ruth	$3,500	$1,500	$500	~
Casey Stengel	$750	$250	$50	$100
Pie Traynor	$1,000	$400	$100	$550
Willie Wells	$1,000	$500	$150	~
Honus Wagner	$2,500	$1,000	$300	~
Hoyt Wilhelm	$45	$20	$10	$12
Cy Young	$2,400	$1,000	$300	~

Autographed Baseballs

With a minimum of foresight an autographed baseball can last several generations before, like an old soldier, it gradually fades away. For a baseball to survive the following rules should be observed:

1. Don't have it signed with a Sharpie. Use a Bic ballpoint.
2. If at all possible, make it an official American or National

League baseball because of the quality of the leather. Balls given out at "ball days" at parks are best used for playing catch and worst used for having autographed.

3. Keep the ball out of any exposure to direct sunlight.
4. If you put it in a holder, periodically take it out and rotate it.
5. Keep in mind that no matter what you do, balls sometimes yellow, spot, or darken over time. These problems are outside your realm of control.
6. To ensure maximum value of the baseball, give some thought to the individuals you have sign the baseball. We have a friend who sat in front of Hall of Famer George Sisler at a game he was scouting in St. Louis in the late 1960s. In addition to Sisler, he had Nelson Briles and Mike Shannon sign it. The addition of Briles and Shannon turned a $1,500—2,000 ball into a $400—500 one (maybe).
7. Do not add any shellac or sealant to the baseball to preserve the signatures. Eventually shellac will darken and crack.
8. The area of the ball where you have the signatures placed is important. If you are working on a Hall of Fame baseball, get someone other than Gaylord Perry or Billy Williams on the "sweet spot". The sweet spot is usually reserved for a player with the stature of a Stan Musial, Joe DiMaggio, or Ted Williams.
9. Personalizations generally detract from the value of a ball by as much as 50–70%, but if you are collecting for the joy of it rather than the investment potential, personalizations add a positive touch and are probably more meaningful. We guarantee you that somewhere out there is a baseball or picture from Babe Ruth personalized to someone with your first name. Finding the picture can be one problem and paying for it another.

Private Signings

The number of private signings has increased significantly as the costs of promoting shows have continued to escalate. A private signing takes place when a promoter employs an athlete or celebrity to sign a predetermined number of autographs at a specified time and place for a fee.

The promoter usually makes it as convenient and comfortable as possible for the autograph guest in a hotel suite stocked with the guest's choice of food and drink.

The private signing is advertised in national publications like *Sports Collectors Digest* or through mailing lists and the costs to sign a variety of items are listed. The promoter also has his own bats, balls, photographs, hats, or helmets in numerous sizes that can be ordered or the collector can send in his items to be autographed. Some promoters offer personalizations for an additional fee of $5 to $20 per item.

Many of the guests who do private signings prefer them to the circus atmosphere of the card and memorabilia show. The amount of money they receive is comparable and the atmosphere is much more conducive to business. The promoter comes to them and they don't have to travel to another city for a show.

Private signings provide collectors with the opportunity to have their items signed by many players who are not on the normal autograph circuit. As player salaries spiral upward, fewer major stars will do shows and turn more to private signings.

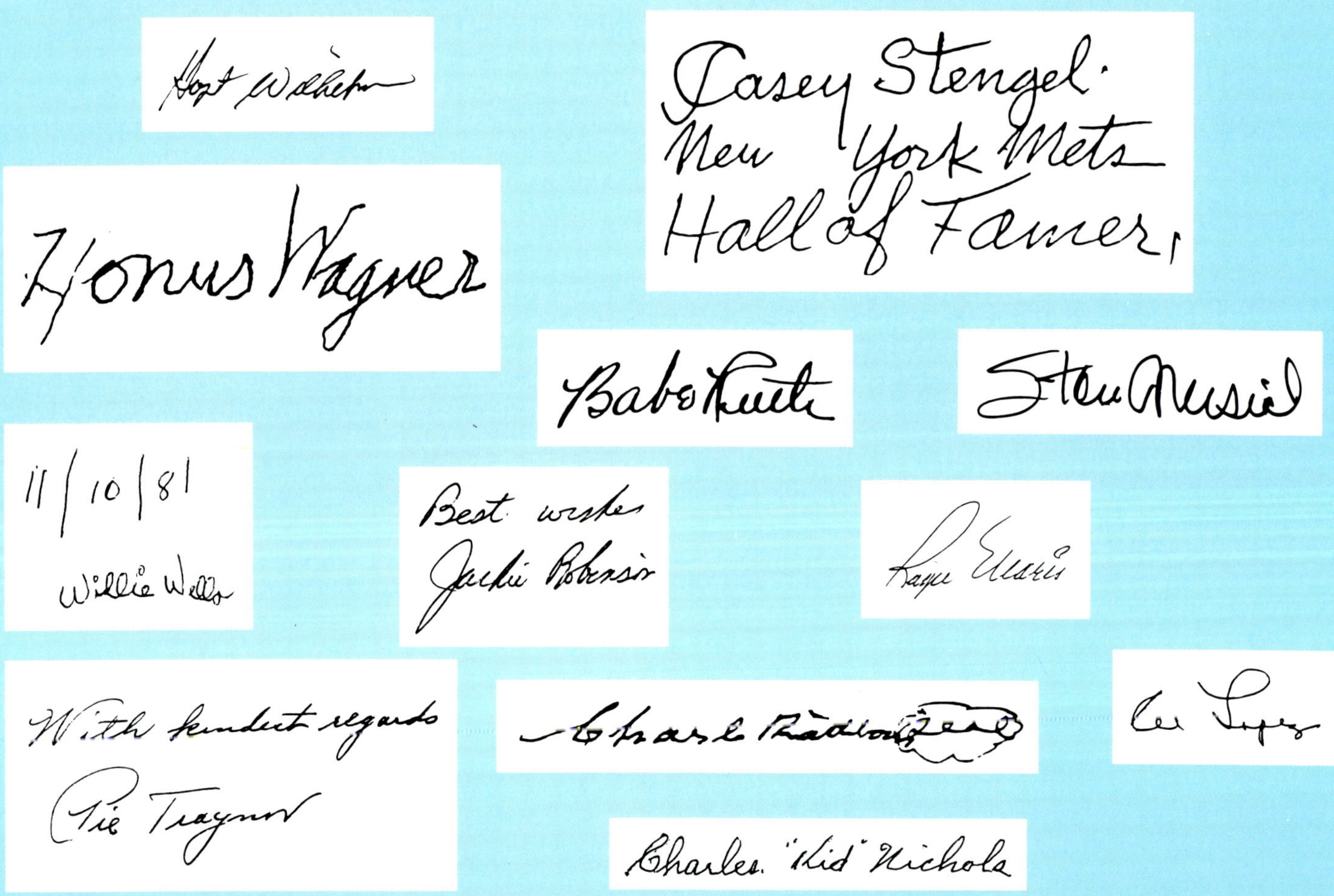

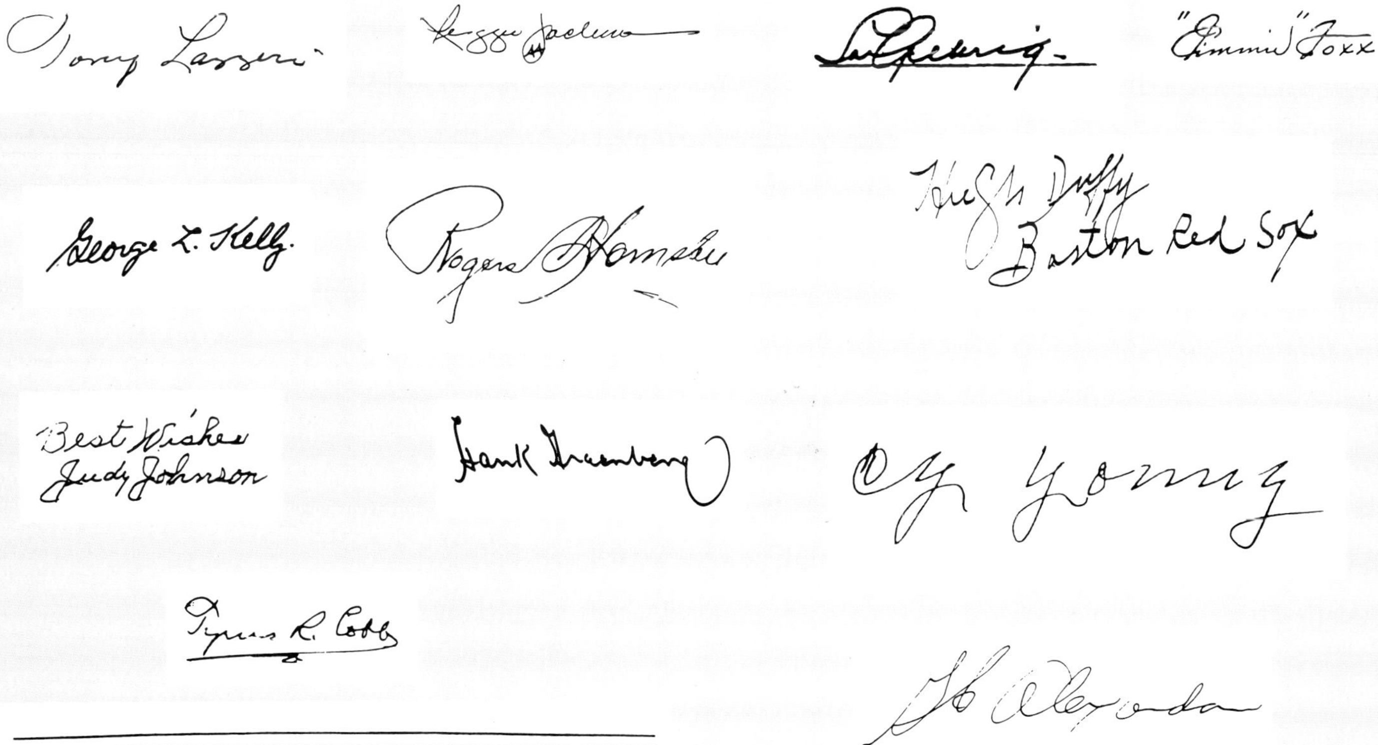

Card, Autograph, & Memorabilia Shows

Baseball card shows with autograph guests probably peaked in popularity in the mid to late 1980s. The success was largely fueled by the collecting public's demand for baseball cards. The autograph guests provided those attending the show another reason to come and for $4–10, depending upon the magnitude of the player, they could add a signature to their baseball or 8 x 10 photograph.

During this period, we attended shows where Joe DiMaggio charged $10 and Mickey Mantle and Whitey Ford were $12 on a "combo" ticket. Mantle would also sign your bat for the same fee. Following his death, autographed Mantle bats were advertised for considerably more than $1,000.

The promoter of the show has significant expenses in staging an event. These would include renting a facility, renting tables and a sound system, hiring security and ticket sellers, advertising locally and nationally, and hiring an autograph guest (or guests). Furthermore, once guests agree to the show, the promoter must then pay the guests' airfare, lodging, and food and drinking expenses, and possibly pick up the tab for their wives, girlfriends, bodyguards, or agents.

The autograph guest is usually paid for his time on a hourly basis or for a predetermined number of signatures. If he is contracted to sign 1,000 autographs and only 700 are sold, the dealer often has a quantity of baseballs or 8 x 10 photographs signed that he can later sell at his future shows or wholesale to his dealers.

The show promoter's income is largely derived from the sale of dealer space to his exhibitors, the sale of admission tickets, the sale of baseballs or 8 x 10 photographs at the admission table, mail-in orders for autographs, and the possibility of receiving a percentage of the food sales at the show from the owner of the facility.

Menu from DiMaggio's Restaurant and Cocktail Lounge, c. late 1940s. $100–125

As the interest in baseball cards continues to decline, the promoter is often hard-pressed to have profitable shows without an "impressive" roster of autograph guests. "Impressive" guests (who have not visited every hamlet in America with a street light) are expensive. The promoter is putting a great deal of his or her money at risk to produce a high profile event that could be a failure.

We have been to shows where there were power failures, weather that kept the crowd away, and advertised guests who didn't show up or were two hours late. All of these potential problems can be expensive for the show promoter and completely outside his or her control.

Autograph guests can be mean-spirited, gracious, drunk, surly, late, and talkative. If the player is being paid by the hour, the talkative guest who poses for pictures, shakes each hand, and answers every question can cost the promoter a considerable amount of money and devour the profits.

We had the misfortune to attend a show in Peoria, Illinois held at an antiques mall with Willie Mays as the guest. Mays and the promoter had apparently failed to discuss the former Giant slugger's philosophy about autographing bats. Shortly after the doors opened and a long line of collectors formed with autograph tickets in hand, Mays put down his Sharpie and walked out the door. The promoter still had his expenses to pay for rent and advertising but the crowd and most of the dealers followed the Say Hey Kid out the door five minutes later. Willie Mays had refused to play in Peoria.

American League baseball signed on the "sweet spot" by Joe DiMaggio—$175. Collectors should keep in mind that there is a huge amount of autographed balls, cards, and pictures that have been stored away in anticipation of long term gains. DiMaggio was one of the first former players to control the number and price of bats that he would sign. Signed DiMaggio bats are much rarer than almost anything else he could have signed.

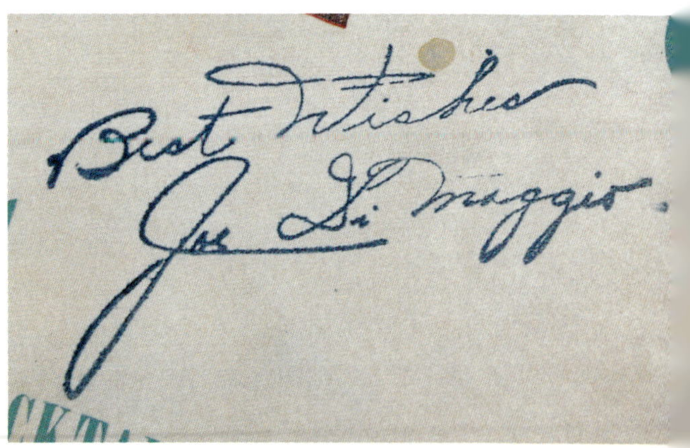

The DiMaggio menu has a stamped autograph of Joe DiMaggio. An actual vintage signature of the Yankee Clipper would add approximately $200 to the value of the menu.

Joe Cronin (d. 1984) autographed this baseball with many of his Red Sox teammates in 1941. $1,000

American League baseball autographed 12 times by Walt Dropo, $100. Dropo shares the major league record for consecutive hits with 12 on July 14 and 15, 1952 while playing for the Red Sox. He signed this baseball 12 times in Cooperstown in 1994.

Baseball autographed by Cronin in the lobby of the Otesaga Hotel in Cooperstown on August 1, 1982. Compare the two Cronin signatures that were signed 41 years apart and they are remarkably similar.

Stan Musial signature on the "sweet spot" of a baseball signed by 11 other members of the Hall of Fame in Cooperstown in 1982, $300–350. The dot above the "S' was made by Joe Cronin's cigar as he autographed the ball in the lobby of the Otesaga Hotel.

Autograph of Negro League star Judy Johnson on the "cigar" ball.

Baseball autographed by Johnny Mize and Bob Feller in 1984. $65

A "theme" ball could be signed by all the living 300 game winners or the 500 home run hitters. The ball was produced to honor the life of Mickey Mantle following his death. It had been signed by his six pallbearers, Whitey Ford, Bobby Murcer, Yogi Berra, Johnny Blanchard, Hank Bauer, and Moose Skowron. It was also autographed by Bobby Richardson who was involved in the funeral service. $350–400

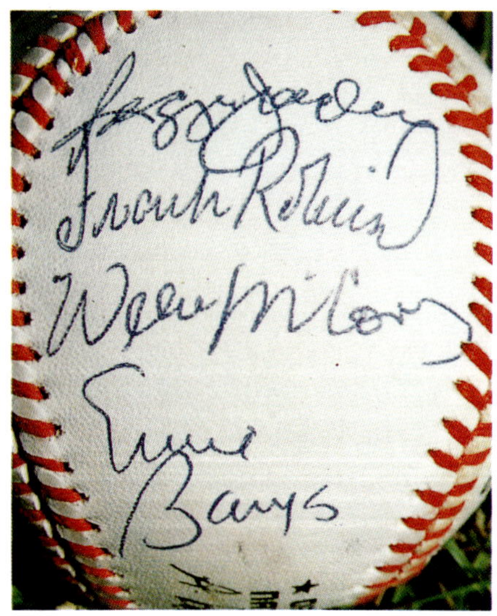

Baseball signed at Atlantic City 500 Home Run Club show in 1989. $800

1941 Red Sox ball with 22 signatures including Williams (sweet spot) and Jimmie Foxx. Williams hit .406 in 1941. $1,000–1400

Jimmie Foxx signature on the 1941 Red Sox ball. We purchased this baseball from a man who had been taken to a Browns–Red Sox double header in St. Louis in 1941 as a child by his aunt. The aunt worked in a hotel where the Red Sox stayed in St. Louis and they attended the game as Foxx's guests.

Hall of Fame baseball signed by Buck Leonard (before his stroke) and Happy Chandler on the sweet spot. There are 17 signatures on the baseball. $400

Hoyt Wilhelm, Brooks Robinson, George Kell, and Monte Irvin are on this panel of the baseball with blue sharpie autographs that have remained crisp.

Ideally, the baseball would have been signed in ballpoint with Hank Aaron and Stan Musial on the sweet spot rather than Leonard and Chandler.

The same baseball was also signed by Burleigh Grimes, Billy Herman, Duke Snider, and Judy Johnson. Grimes is one of the more difficult signatures from those who could have signed after 1980.

Signature of Fay Vincent

Baseball signed by Ted Williams and Bill Terry. Terry was the last National League player to hit over .400 (1930) and Williams was the last in the American League (1941). $375

In 1986 Michael Jordan came to Normal, Illinois to play in an exhibition charity basketball game at Illinois State University's Horton Fieldhouse. The morning of the game Jordan appeared at a local Chevrolet dealership to sign autographs. Approximately 17 people showed up to get anything they wanted signed by Jordan. He graciously signed a National League baseball for us. $300–375

Autograph of Bill Terry (d. 1989)

Perhaps one of the greatest players you have never heard of is Cecil Travis of the Washington Senators. Travis had a lifetime batting average of .314 as a shortstop with the Washington Senators. In 1941 he hit .359 with 218 hits and 101 runs batted in. He spent 1942–1944 in the military during World War II and returned to play portions of three more seasons before retiring. At some distant point Cecil Travis will be elected by the veteran's committee to the Hall of Fame. A single-signed Cecil Travis ball is presently worth about $50. When he is finally elected to the Hall of Fame it will be worth considerably more.

At a cocktail party at the Otesaga Hotel in Cooperstown on July 30, 1988, we had the unique opportunity to secure the autographs of five men who at one point or another served as commissioner of baseball. A. Bartlett Giamatti, Bowie Kuhn, Fay Vincent, Peter Ueberroth, and Happy Chandler signed the baseball. $500

As a child, Pete Gray lost an arm in an accident. He overcame this physical setback to play a single season with the St. Louis Browns in 1945 and hit .218 in 234 at bats. A single-signed Pete Gray ball is worth $50–75

Signatures of Ueberroth and Kuhn

Baseball autographed on a side panel by President Bill Clinton, $375. If the ball was personalized "to Monica" and signed by Clinton, you could set your own price.

Baseball autographed by former senator and current statesman George Mitchell. $75–100

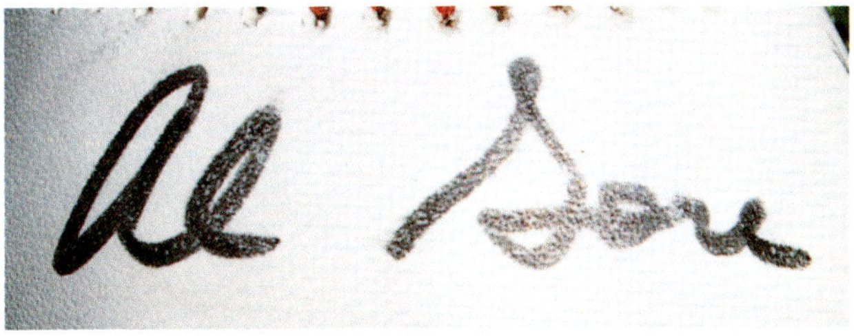

Baseball autographed by Al Gore on the sweet spot. $175

American Girls' Baseball League ball autographed by three former members of the Rockford Peaches. $45

Baseball autographed by Ronald Reagan. $450

The American Girls' league baseball is midway sized between a baseball and a softball. The balls are still being made and are sold at the Hall of Fame gift shop in Cooperstown, selling for about $15.

Baseball autographed by Richard Nixon. $450

American Girls' League box for a baseball. An original ball in its original box would be worth $200–400.

Baseball autographed by Gerald Ford. $225

Baseball personalized and autographed by Jimmy Carter. $150–200

Framed picture of Eddie Cicotte and Ray Schalk who were the opening battery in the 1919 World Series for the White Sox. Included with the photographs of the players is a program used as a prop in the film "Eight Men Out". There are also "cut" signatures of Cicotte and Schalk. $650

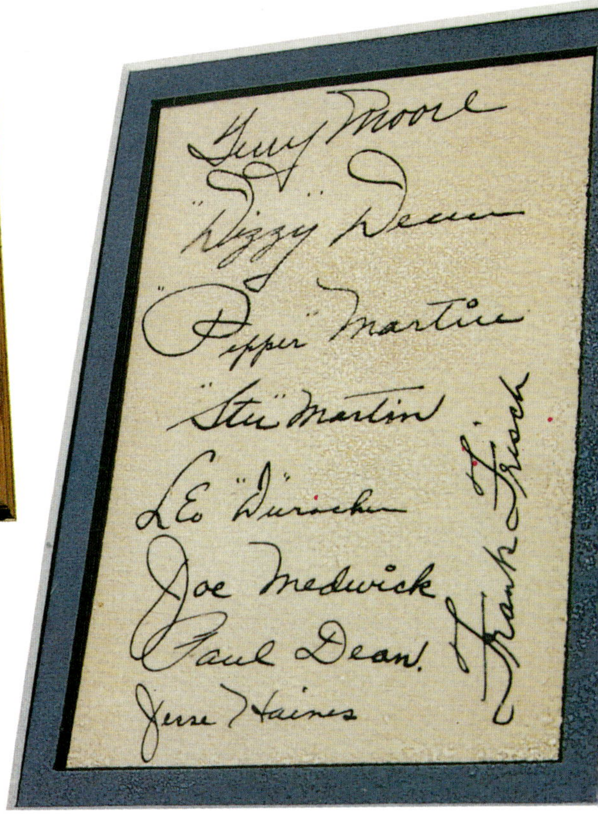

Government postcard signed by 9 members of the Cardinals' "Gas House Gang". Card includes five members of the Hall of Fame—Dizzy Dean, Leo Durocher, Haines, Frank Frisch, and Ducky Medwick. $200–275

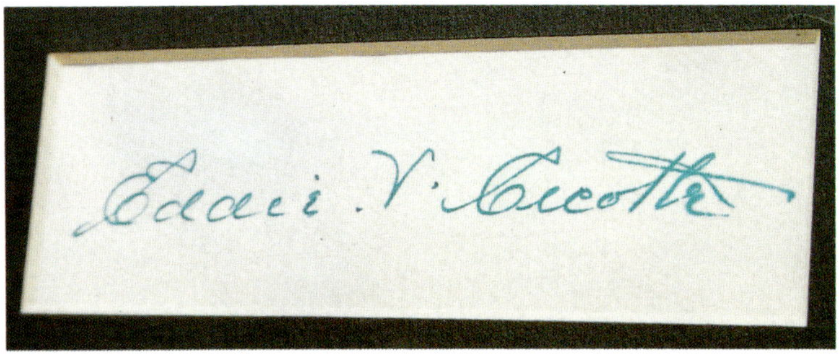

Eddie Cicotte "cut"

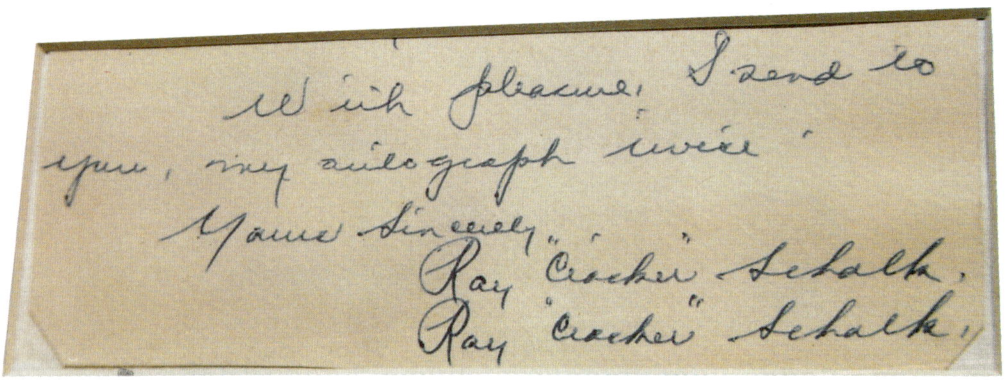

Ray "Cracker" Schalk "cut"

Ty Cobb complete check from 1954. $500

Induction cachet of Reggie Jackson from 1993 with his autograph. $85

Lou Gehrig cachet from June 10, 1989 when the Gehrig stamp was introduced in Cooperstown. Autographed by Ted Williams. $125

Close-up of Ted Williams autograph on the Gehrig cachet.

Framed picture of Mario Cuomo and Bart Giamatti taken on June 10, 1989 while reviewing a parade honoring the Gehrig stamp and the 150th anniversary of the "invention" of baseball in Cooperstown. The Gehrig Hall of Fame plaque has been signed on the reverse by both men. $750

Close-up of autographs on the Gehrig plaque.

Chapter 4

...................Baseball Collectibles

Collecting Chili
by Stew Salowitz

There's a photo in my den that shows me, at age seven, with a San Francisco Giants cap on my head and a baseball bat in my hand. In the more than 35 years since, I have remained a Giants fan, through good teams and bad, over a distance of two time zones and more than 2,100 miles.

I have always collected some kind of Giants' items—media guides, yearbooks, and cards mostly—and while my all-time favorite player is always going to be Willie Mays, since 1981 my favorite "modern" player to follow has been Charles Theodore "Chili" Davis.

Since Davis started out with the Giants and spent more than six seasons with them, it made perfect sense to start collecting specific Chili items since he was on my favorite team. I started collecting Davis' baseball cards very early on because I always got a set of the entire Giants team. It was fairly easy back in the days when it was only Topps, Fleer and Donruss producing cards. But then came Upper Deck, Bowman, Score, Pinnacle, and their variations ("Tiffany", "Traded", "Micro", "Gold"), along with regional sets (Mother's Cookies, for instance)—the influx and surplus of which has complicated the card collecting business as a whole.

Over the years I have been fortunate enough, often with the assistance of Dick Dobbins and his San Francisco Giants memorabilia operation, to obtain some Chili equipment—a hat, batting gloves, wrist band. While I was standing on the field during batting practice in San Francisco one time, former Giant first baseman Dave Bergman helped me get a very new Chili Davis bat. (Other bats came from Kenrich, which older collectors will remember as a top supplier of game-used wood.)

Dobbins also helped me get a Chili Davis black mesh game jersey, used by the team only sparingly in late 1981, along with a batting practice jersey.

I'm not a fan of fantasy baseball because it forces participants to cheer for players not associated with a favorite team. I faced a similar dilemma when Chili left the Giants—being his fan has forced me to follow the boxscores and fortunes of the California Angels (during two different tenures), Minnesota Twins, Kansas City Royals, and now the New York Yankees. His free-agent wandering has also made adding to my Chili collection more challenging.

While Chili was with the Angels, I managed to obtain an Angels jersey and a Chili Davis Starting Lineup figure (an item that was very hard to get and is still sought-after). Through Portland, Oregon dealer Robb Wochnick I acquired one of Chili's seldom-used (really not even broken-in) MacGregor baseball gloves, autographed on a finger by Chili himself.

And while I have no merchandise from Davis' stays with the Twins or Royals, I am not concerned. I know I can never have even one piece of every bit of all the Chili Davis memorabilia there is—I can't even be the best of the collectors of Chili. That honor belongs to a Scottsdale, Arizona man (who shall remain nameless), who has one of Chili's All-Star rings and, from what I understand, a World Series trophy.

I certainly never set out to collect Chili memorabilia with the devotion John Livington of Cleburne, Texas has for Nolan Ryan. In addition to the usual memorabilia like cards, uniform apparel, and such, Livington, whose home is a virtual shrine to Nolan Ryan, has managed to horde oil paintings, pocket knives, and figurines—even a Nolan Ryan chest X-ray.

I set out to do it because it was fun and because he was part of the Giants. As it turns out, I got lucky—not only did Chili play many seasons for San Francisco, but he also became one of the top designated hitters in the American League, so he has given me many years of enjoyment. It would not have been that way if I had chosen Jack Clark or Jeffery Leonard.

Collecting the memorabilia of one player—from any sport—can be especially satisfying if undertaken with not the eye of an investor, but a fan, and as a fun project, maybe even a challenge. In my basement, I have a Johnnie Lemaster Giants gray road jersey and game-used bat. I made those purchases not with the idea that Lemaster, the Giants' shortstop in the 1980s, would one day be in the Hall of Fame and that my memorabilia would skyrocket in value—Lemaster just happened to wear the same jersey number (10) that I always wore, it was a uniform from my favorite team, and it was affordable.

My two-fold advice is simple. Pick a player you can enjoy, hopefully, for a number of years. This is to discourage a person form jumping on the bandwagon of a Chipper Jones or Kerry Wood—if their careers pan out, you'll fight a battle with hundreds of other "speculators" to get their memorabilia at a reasonable price. There are approximately 700 major league players to pick from—maybe you'll get lucky. And I always encourage people to look first on their own favorite team, although with free agents jumping around, it does make it more difficult.

Also, know your limitations and what you can afford. I've never spent a lot a money on obtaining Chili Davis material, yet I have several things I can be proud of, that look good hanging in my den, and are great conversation pieces. I am as proud of my Angels' game programs that have Chili on the cover, because they took some work to unearth and obtain. The hunt to get things is often as enjoyable or more enjoyable as actually having them.

Recently I read that Chili is one of the most difficult baseball autographs to obtain, which should make my collection more "valuable". But I've always thought my collection was *priceless* because of the care I've taken in building it and because it represents a player who has given me years of entertainment, despite labor strife and other problems, in the best sport in America.

Game-worn wrist band form the Giants. $15–20

Game-used Chili Davis glove. $225–275

Game-worn batting gloves from the San Francisco Giants. $25–40 (pair)

Game-worn jersey from the Giants. $250–300

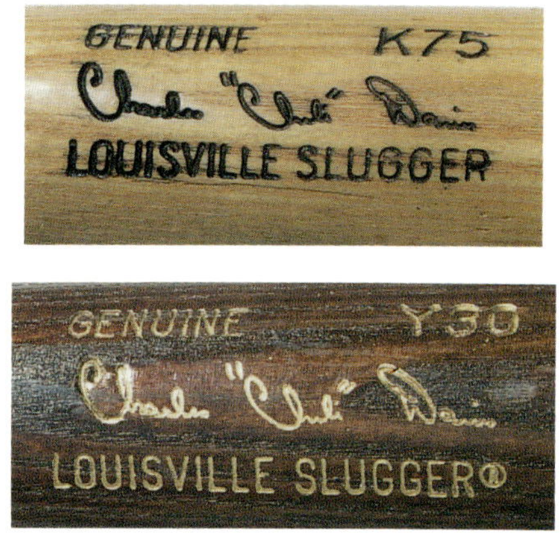

Game-used bats. $95–115 (each)

"Chili 3" license plates from Illinois, c. 1998

Hall of Fame Press Pins

The baseball Hall of Fame has issued press pins to its staff, guests, and the media during the Induction Weekend since 1982. It is not an uncommon sight to see individuals wearing a pin stopped on the streets of Cooperstown and offered varying amounts of money for their gift from the Hall of Fame.

1997 pin (Fox, Niekro, Lasorda, Wells) $275–325

1996 pin (Foster, Weaver, Hanlon, Bunning) $275–325

1995 pin (Hulbert, Willis, Schmidt, Ashburn, Day) $300–375

1992 pin (Seaver, Fingers, Newhouser, McGowan) $325–375

1987 pin (Billy Williams, Hunter, Dandridge) $400–450

1990 pin (Morgan, Palmer) $400–475

1986 pin (Lombardi, McCovey, Doerr) $350–375

Gold Hall of Fame Plaques

Since the late 1930s several companies have produced Hall of Fame postcards that depict the plaques of the members. Included in a list of companies would be Albertype, Artvue, Dexter, Curteichcolor, Mike Roberts, and Scenic Art.

The gold or yellow Hall of Fame plaques have been offered for sale by the Hall of Fame since the mid-1960s. Nationally known autograph collector and dealer Ron Gordon wrote in 1987:

> In my opinion it's harder to complete a set of autographed gold plaques than it is to complete a set of unsigned 1952 Topps or unsigned 1933 Goudey cards. If you have unlimited funds and set out to complete either card set or a set of gold plaques, I think you would complete the cards first. Demand in the past few years alone for the signed plaques has caused the supply of a few of them to dry up the point they are seldom offered in the hobby.

The plaques can be ordered individually or in a complete set from the Hall of Fame gift shop in Cooperstown. You will find that the plaques are considerably easier to acquire than the autographs on them.

Rumors

There have been stories over the years that George Weiss signed some plaques in his hospital room prior to his death in August of 1972. The current consensus of opinion is that the Weiss plaques that were autographed probably were signed by someone other than Weiss. One of his nurses is usually credited with the mysterious signature.

Paul Waner and Bill McKechnie also turn up on some lists of possible signers but Waner and McKechnie probably did not sign any of the gold plaques.

Variations

The only player in the Hall of Fame with two distinctly different gold plaques is Ted Williams. Williams had the picture on his plaque redone in the mid-1980s. His Hall of Fame cards now reflect that change.

Members of the Hall of Fame Who Could Have Signed Gold Hall of Fame Plaques

Henry Aaron
Walter Alston*
Luis Aparicio
Luke Appling*
Richie Ashburn*
Earl Averill*
Dave Bancroft*
Ernie Banks
Al Barlick*
Cool Papa Bell*
Johnny Bench
Yogi Berra
Lou Boudreau
Lou Brock
Jim Bunning
Roy Campanella**
Rod Carew
Max Carey*
Steve Carlton
Happy Chandler*
Earle Combs*
Jocko Conlan*
Stan Coveleski*
Sam Crawford*
Joe Cronin*
Ray Dandridge*
Dizzy Dean*
Bill Dickey*
Joe DiMaggio
Bobby Doerr
Don Drysdale*
Red Faber*
Bob Feller
Rick Ferrell*
Rollie Fingers
Elmer Flick*
Whitey Ford
Jimmie Foxx*
Frank Frisch*
Charlie Gehringer*
Bob Gibson
Lefty Gomez*
Goose Goslin*
Hank Greenberg*
Burleigh Grimes*
Lefty Grove*
Chick Hafey*
Jesse Haines*
Bucky Harris*
Gabby Hartnett*
Billy Herman*
Harry Hooper*
Waite Hoyt*
Cal Hubbard*
Carl Hubbell*
Catfish Hunter
Monte Irvin
Reggie Jackson
Travis Jackson*
Ferguson Jenkins
Judy Johnson*
Al Kaline
George Kell
George Kelly*
Harmon Killebrew
Ralph Kiner
Sandy Koufax
Tommy Lasorda
Bob Lemon
Buck Leonard*
Fred Lindstrom*
Al Lopez
Ted Lyons
Lee MacPhail
Mickey Mantle*
Heinie Manush*
Juan Marichal
Rube Marquard*
Eddie Mathews
Willie Mays
Joe McCarthy*
Willie McCovey
Joe Medwick*
Johnny Mize*
Joe Morgan
Stan Musial
Hal Newhouser*
Phil Niekro
Satchel Paige*
Jim Palmer
Gaylord Perry
Pee Wee Reese
Sam Rice*
Phil Rizzuto
Robin Roberts
Brooks Robinson
Frank Robinson
Jackie Robinson*
Edd Roush*
Red Ruffing*
Ray Schalk*
Mike Schmidt
Red Schoendienst
Tom Seaver
Joe Sewell*
George Sisler*
Enos Slaughter
Duke Snider
Warren Spahn
Willie Stargell
Casey Stengel*
Don Sutton
Bill Terry*
Pie Traynor*
Lloyd Waner*
Earl Weaver
Zack Wheat*
Hoyt Wilhelm
Billy Williams
Ted Williams
Early Wynn
Carl Yastrzemski

* deceased

** Campanella signed with the assistance of a mechanical device because of complications from an automobile accident that left him physically disabled.

By our calculations there are 122 members of the Hall of Fame who could have signed the gold plaques through the 1998 Induction.

The Rarest Autographed Gold Hall of Fame Plaques

The 10 most difficult autographed gold or yellow Hall of Fame plaques are:

Jimmie Foxx
Goose Goslin ("front signed")
Dave Bancroft
Sam Crawford
Cal Hubbard
Jackie Robinson
Elmer Flick
Ray Schalk
Bucky Harris
Walter Alston—The window of opportunity was very limited for Alston to sign as he died within three months of his induction in 1984. He was too ill to attend the ceremonies in Cooperstown, so any plaques that he autographed were acquired directly from him or through the mail.

Lists

When lists of autographed Hall of Fame plaques appear, the descriptive term "pre-stroke" is used for some for the plaques signed by Carl Hubbell and Buck Leonard. Following their strokes the quality of their signatures, as you might expect, declined. Leonard learned to sign with his left hand after his stroke. The earlier "pre-stroke" signatures are always $5-10 more expensive per plaque.

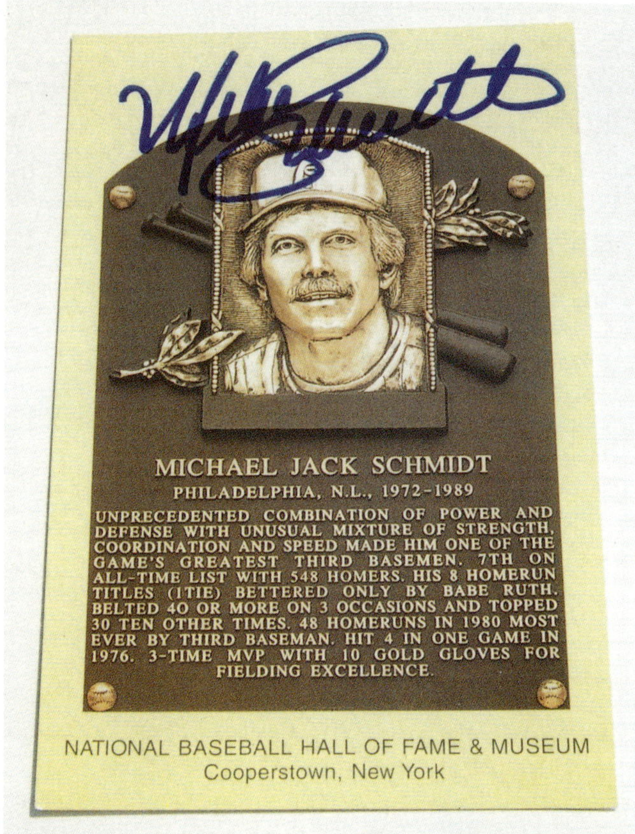

Mike Schmidt. $55

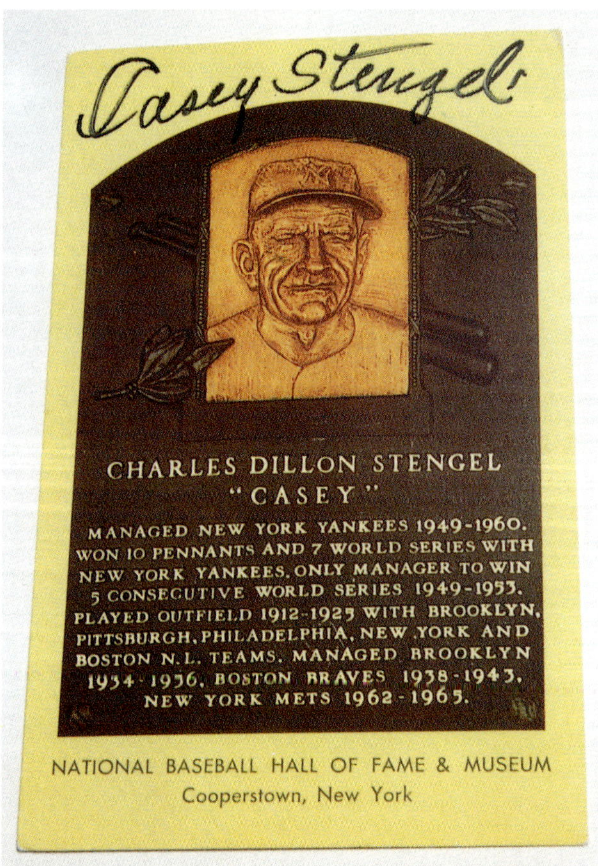

Casey Stengel (d. 1975). $125

Satchel Paige business card and plaque. $150

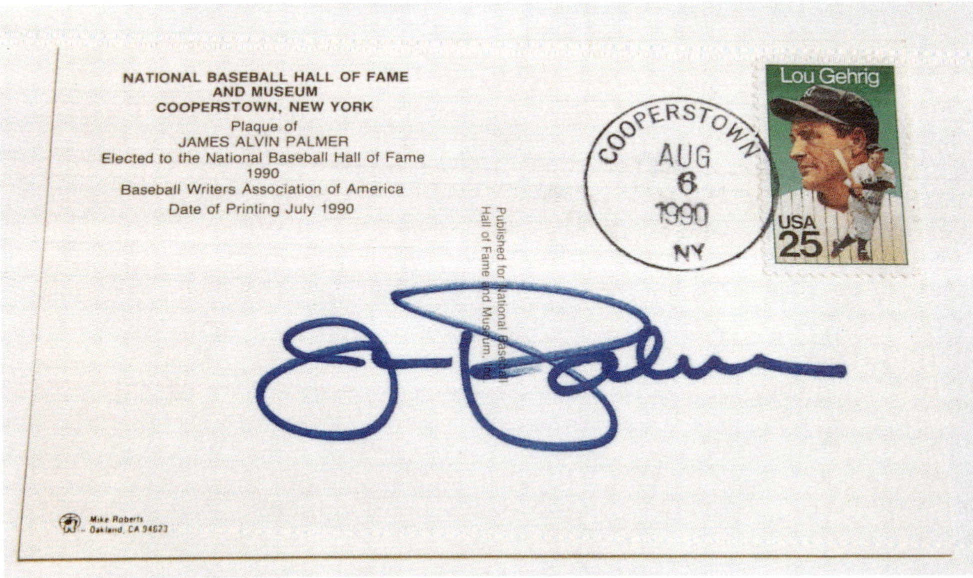

Jim Palmer plaque signed and postmarked on his induction day. $50

Reggie Jackson. $40

Joe Sewell (d. 1990). $30

Red Schoendienst. $20

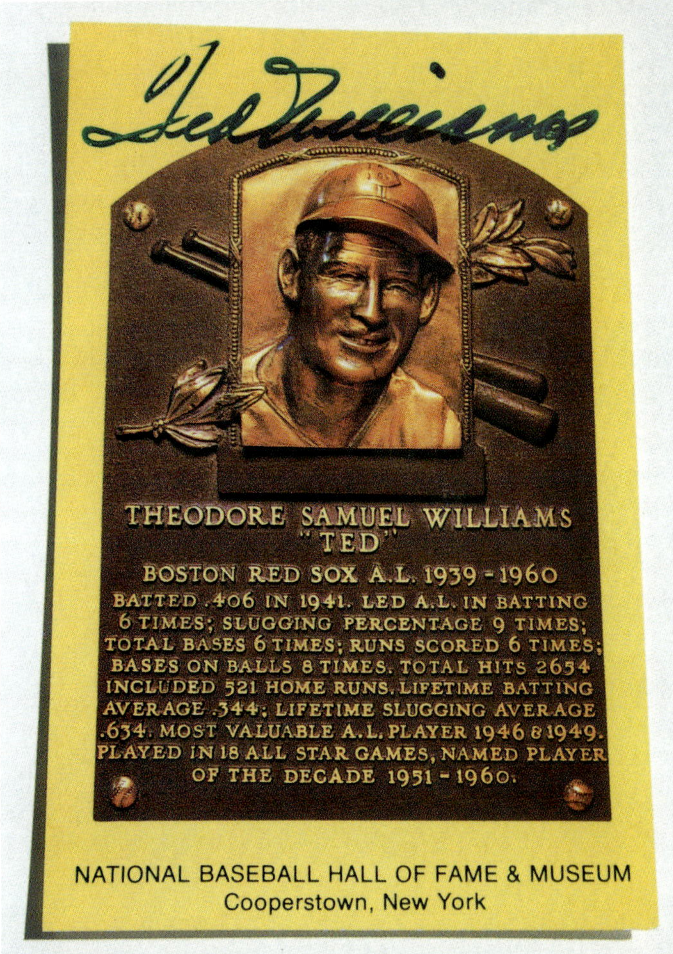

Ted Williams. $250

Charlie Gehringer (d. 1993). $30

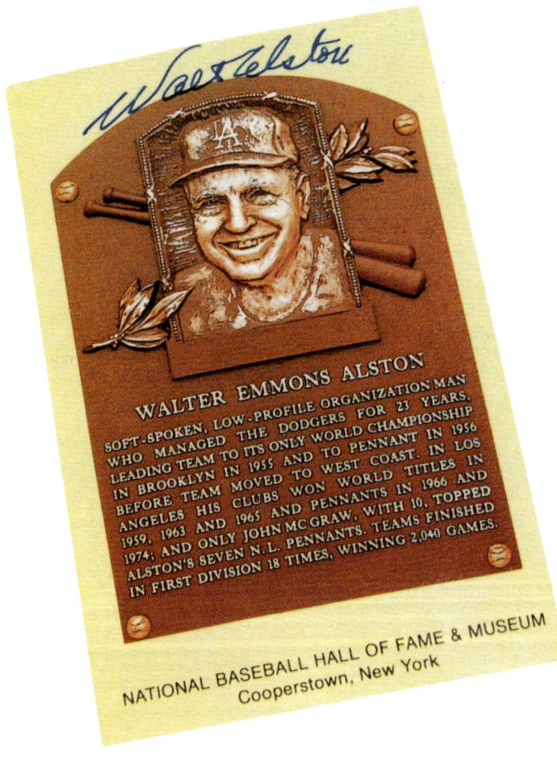

Walter Alston (d. 1984). $200

Burleigh Grimes (d. 1985). $35

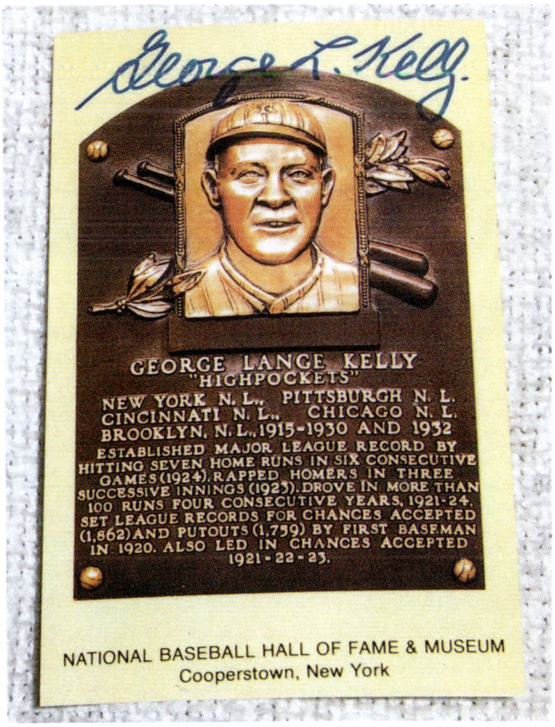

George Kelly (d. 1984). $35

Al Lopez. $45

Buck Leonard (d. 1997). $35

Ford Frick (d. 1978). $110

Investment Potential of Baseball Collectibles

Shows

Periodically there is a "mega theme" autograph show somewhere in America that brings together the 3000 hit club, 500 homerun club, Heisman Trophy winners, or the Super Bowl MVPs. The promoter always offers by mail a bat, ball, poster, helmet, or lithograph signed by all the attendees.

Since the first 500 homerun show in Atlantic City, Mickey Mantle has died and Ted Williams no longer signs many baseballs. The value of a ball from that show has increased dramatically.

Signed items from these shows will always be a sound investment because they are difficult to repeat with the same guests due to the inevitable: death, sickness, infirmity, or the inability to get everybody involved under contract.

Baseballs

Single-signed baseballs from Hall of Famers Leon Day, Leo Durocher, Richie Ashburn, and Lee MacPhail are still affordable and should be added to a collection as soon as the opportunity presents itself. They are going to increase in value.

Hall of Fame Plaques

Autographed Hall of Fame plaques (yellow) are generally underpriced and certainly underappreciated. How many people if given the chance to secure an autograph from Ted Williams got it on a Hall of Fame plaque? Our guess is that a ball, bat, cap, book, or picture took preference over a Hall of Fame plaque.

"Upper End" Memorabilia

Over the years, quality "upper end" pieces of baseball memorabilia with a strong provenance or history of ownership have been exceptional investments. More common "lower end" examples historically have not risen in value with the same intensity.

Uniforms

If a collector-investor can purchase a jersey of a "sure" member of the Hall of Fame before his career is over, it usually turns out to be considerably less expensive than after his election to the Cooperstown shrine. What is costing $600–900 can turn into several thousand after the five-year waiting period is completed.

10 Suggestions for Semi-Serious Baseball Collectors

1. If the red light is on at the Krispy Kreme on your way to the card show, stop.
2. Buy a set of Topps baseball cards each year and put them away for a better day. It will come.
3. When the baseball card market appears to have absolutely bottomed out, buy some and put them under the bed.
4. The only thing Bob Feller, Enos Slaughter, and Warren Spahn have not signed is your tax return.
5. The 18 "anniversary" Hartlands with their original boxes will continue each year to increase gradually in price. The "Dallas" Hartlands will be an even better long term investment.
6. Game worn jerseys of "common" players are not good investments. In the future fans will care less about these players than they do now. If the jersey is being purchased to wear or hang on a wall and it is priced at less than $125, give it some consideration. You may be reasonably sure it is legitimate. If the name on the back of the Philadelphia jersey is "Schmidt" rather then "Amaro" and it's $125, we would be more than a little concerned about its authenticity.
7. When a card or memorabilia show advertises "free" autographs, be prepared to wait in a long line and bring your lunch. The guy in front of you will be sure to provide an hour's worth of entertainment discussing the significance of his collection. By the time you make your way to the front of the line, the individual signing the free autographs will be gone.
8. Autographed baseballs, like some pieces of art, increase significantly following the demise of the individual who signed it. In the 1980s Johnny Mize was a cordial guest at a hundred shows and charged $5 for his signature. Recently we have seen single-signed Mize baseballs for $65-75. That may still be a little high, but it is a pretty good short term investment.
9. Send a baseball to the president of the National League, American League, and the commissioner. You can use the addresses we provided in the Sources section of this book. Include a self-addressed and stamped return container (large envelope or Priority Mail envelope with $3 postage). They will usually sign the baseball at no charge and return it to you. Commissioners and league presidents do not do shows and are not "easy" autographs.
10. Take the "what's it worth" line out of your vocabulary and collect baseball memorabilia because you enjoy it.

Reach Official Major League baseball with William Harridge as president. Harridge served the American League from 1931 through the 1958 season. $100–150 in original wrapping

Single-signed Babe Ruth baseball. This baseball was purchased from a Florida physician who had accepted it from a patient as payment for services. The ball had been in a lock box for the thirty years until the doctor decided to sell it. The Ruth signature on the unofficial ball probably dates from the early 1940s. Ruth died in 1948. $2000–2800

A portion of the crowd at the games in "The Natural" were actually life-sized photographs mounted on particle board and tied to the seats. Unlike the actors, they did not require a per diem or periodic coffee breaks. They also were always on time and refrained from temper tantrums. $75–100 (each)

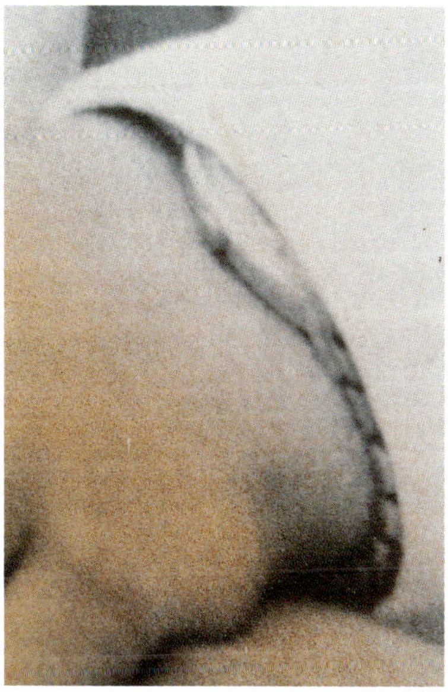

The younger man has on a watch that didn't exist in 1939.

Ted Williams Moxie advertisement from the 1950s. This cardboard "stand-up" was used on a counter to assist Moxie sales in grocery stores. $650–1000

Ted Williams Moxie "stand-up" or counter display, c. 1950s. $650–1000

Ty Cobb calendar from 1954, 12" x 7". $275–300

Coffee cup and soup bowl from Mickey Mantle's Country Cookin' restaurant, c. 1950s. $100

The Brown and Bigelow Company of St. Paul, Minnesota offered advertisers the opportunity to put their name on a series of baseball calendars that were produced between 1950 and 1969. Each calendar contained a scene involving a member of the Hall of Fame providing direction or instruction to a child or a group of children. The baseball art was also available on items ranging from playing cards to ink blotters.

Framed KHOW (Denver) picture of Mickey Cochrane—$300

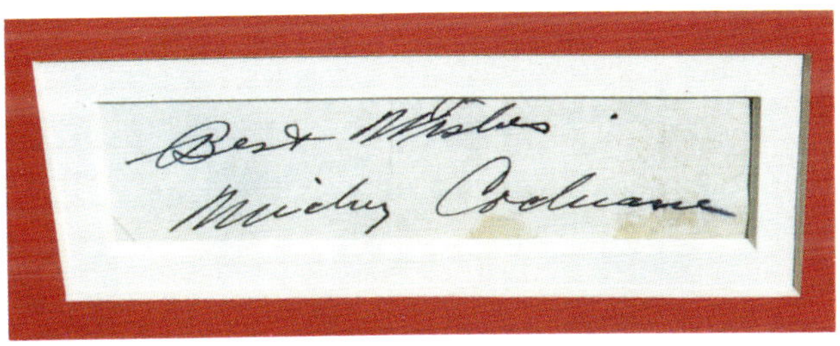

Cochrane's autograph

Honus Wagner poster from Morton Grove, Illinois, 24" x 36". $300–400

1952 Connie Mack Calendar, 34" x 16 ½". $200–275

Joe DiMaggio calendar from 1957, 8" x 11". $250–325

Frank Frisch calendar from 1958, 34" x 16 ½". $400–550

John McGraw calendar from 1953, 10" x 17 ½", $225–250. The calendars are especially difficult to find in excellent to mint condition without all of the months torn away.

Ty Cobb playing cards from 1954. $65–75 per deck

Ty Cobb box for the cards

1952 box of Connie Mack cards given out by the Philadelphia A's. $125–175

Close-up of Philadelphia A's box for holding two decks of cards

Joe Tinker Club House Cigars box, c. 1915. $350–425

Babe Ruth All America Athletic Underwear box, c. 1925. $375–400

Big Six Union Suits box, c. 1915, $65–100. Christy Mathewson (d. 1925) won 37 games in 1908 for the New York Giants and was nicknamed "Big Six" because he was almost 6'2" tall in an era when most major league players were 5'9". The Big Six Union Suit people capitalized on Mathewson's celebrity without paying him an endorsement fee. If Mathewson's picture or name was on the box it would be worth considerably more than $65–100.

Side of the box showing Ruth's printed autograph and close up.

Unopened can of the short-lived Holy Cow Root Beer with Harry Carey's image, c. early 1990s. $6

Six pack of Ted's Root Beer, c. 1950s. The drink was not a major mrketing triumph and relatively few cartons and bottles have survived. The bottle caps, as you would guess, are even rarer. $400–500

Adhesive-backed advertisement for Ted's Creamy Root Beer, to be applied to a glass door or freezer. 9" x 4 ½", c. 1950s. $15–20

32 ounce bottle of Moxie with Ted Williams label, c. 1950s. $30–45

Official League Ball radio in working order, c. 1940. $750–1000

1951 Pirates yearbook, $150–175. This yearbook is of special interest to collectors because it was the first one issued by the Pirates. The Pirates finished with a record of 64-90 in 1951 and there was not a great deal of demand for the yearbook, so relatively few have survived.

The 1952 Pirates (42-112) are considered one of the worst teams in the history of baseball. The 1952 yearbook has a colorful cover and sold fewer copies than the 1951 version. $100–125

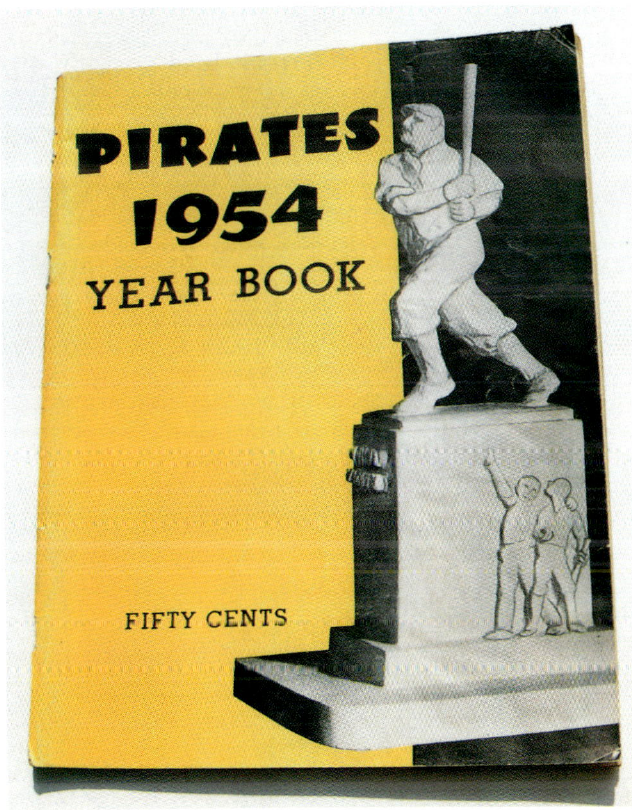

The 1954 Pirates finished with a record of 53-101. The highlight of the season was putting the proposed Honus Wagner statue on the front of the yearbook. $50–75

The 1958 Pirates improved to a record of 84-70 and finished second to the Braves in the National League. Interest was up and the demand for the yearbook increased proportionately. $35–50

Baltimore Orioles Surf book from 1987, $50–60. The first printing of Surf books took place in March of 1987 with 26 major league teams taking part. The project was sponsored by Surf laundry detergent and contained the Topps baseball cards from 1952-1986. The books were to be passed out at major league parks in a marketing program. The Orioles' books were only handed to patrons at a minor league park in Charlotte, North Carolina, and are the rarest of the Surf books. Most Surf books can still be purchased for $2-6. In 1987–88 they were worth a whole lot more when collectors were swept in a miniature Surf book mania.

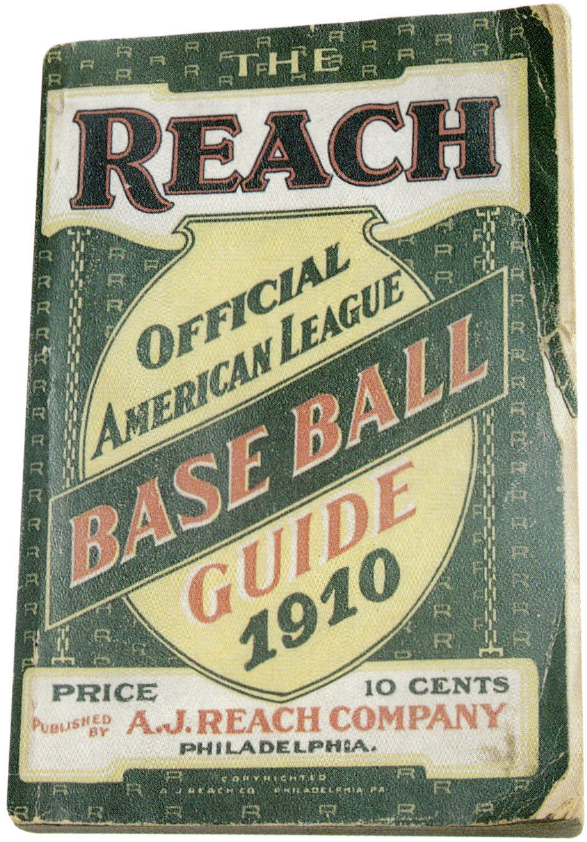

Reach American League Baseball Guide for 1910, $45–55. The back of the 1910 Reach Guide shows what the American League baseball looked like during that period. The first season in which a league president's signature appeared on a baseball was in 1934 with John Heydler on the National League version. In 1935 William Harridge added his imprinted signature to the American League baseball.

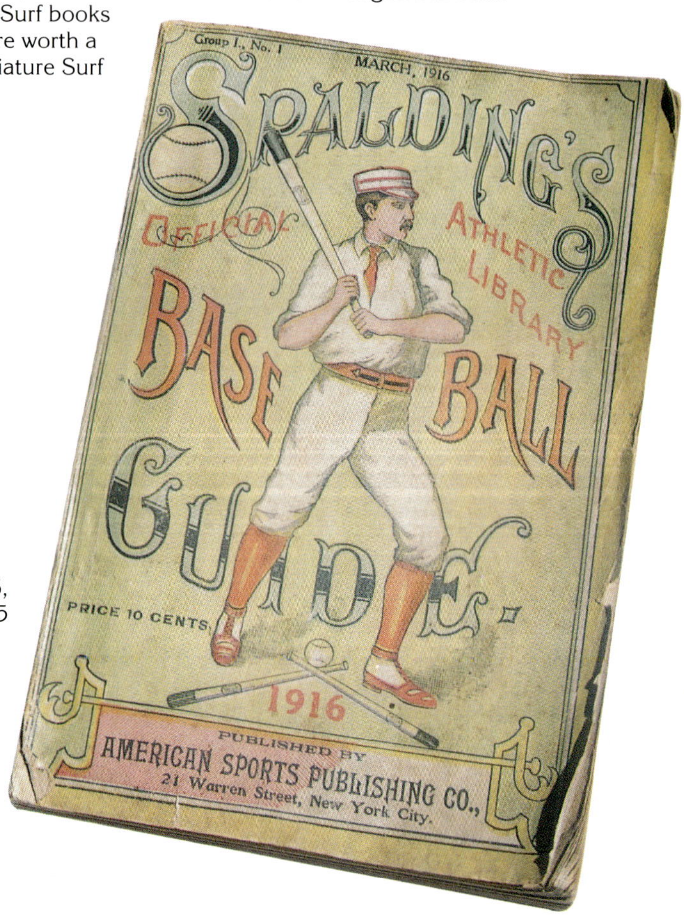

Spalding's Base Ball Guide for 1916, average condition. $35–45

Back of the 1916 guide showing the National League baseball.

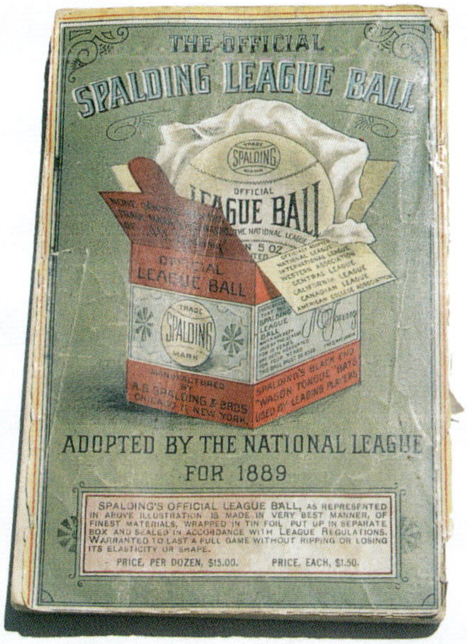

Back of 1889 guide showing the Spalding League Ball "adopted by the National League for 1889".

Hardbound copy of *Our Base Ball Club and How It Won the Championship* by Noah Brooks, with an introduction by Al G. Spalding, published in 1884. $135–175. This book by Noah Brooks is considered to be the first full-length fictional book about baseball ever published. If it was an autographed copy signed by Brooks and Albert Spalding, it would be worth $4000–5000.

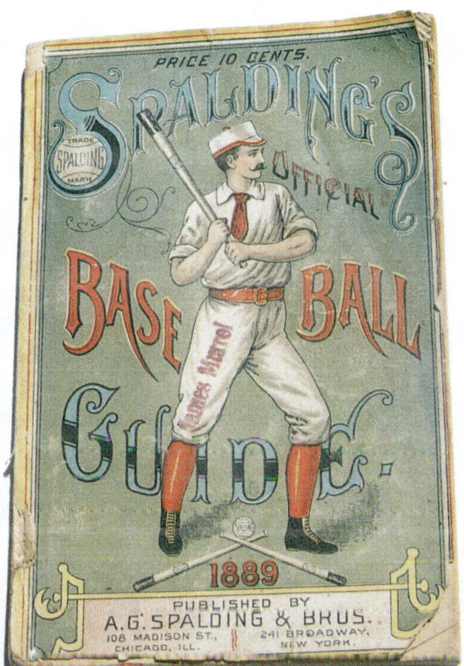

Rare Spalding's Base Ball Guide for 1889. $150–200

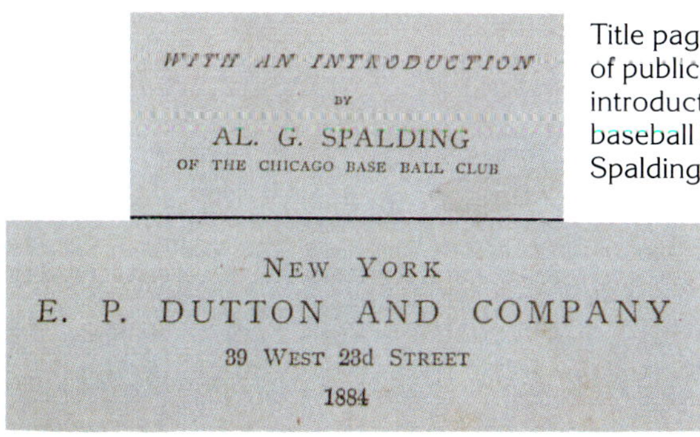
WITH AN INTRODUCTION
BY
AL. G. SPALDING
OF THE CHICAGO BASE BALL CLUB

NEW YORK
E. P. DUTTON AND COMPANY
39 WEST 23d STREET
1884

Title page showing date of publication and introduction written by baseball legend Albert Spalding.

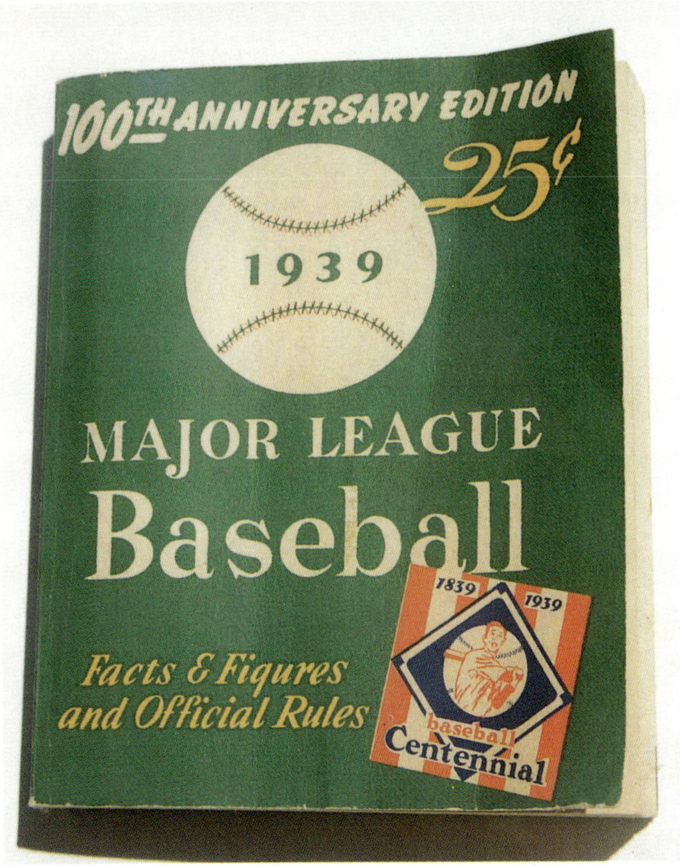

Major league baseball guide published in 1939. $20–35

Seat from Crosley Field in Cincinnati. $500

Cardinal pennant on a stick, sold at the park, c. 1940s. $20–25

Cast iron Reds logo on side of the chair.

Reverse of the Giants season pass with inscribed name of Hall of Famer George Kelly (d. 1984). Kelly played with the Giants from 1915–1917 and 1919–1926.

New York Giants sterling silver season's pass for 1926 given to the players, Broadway stars, politicians, and other "glad handers". $600–800

Swatch of flannel from suit ordered by Johnny Bench in 1989. This is a typical high quality swatch of gray flannel with a red stripe until you pay special attention to the pin stripe. It spells out "Johnny Bench".

Federal League doll.

Baggage sticker from the 1931 major league tour of Japan from the estate of Hall of Fame Infielder George Kelly. $40

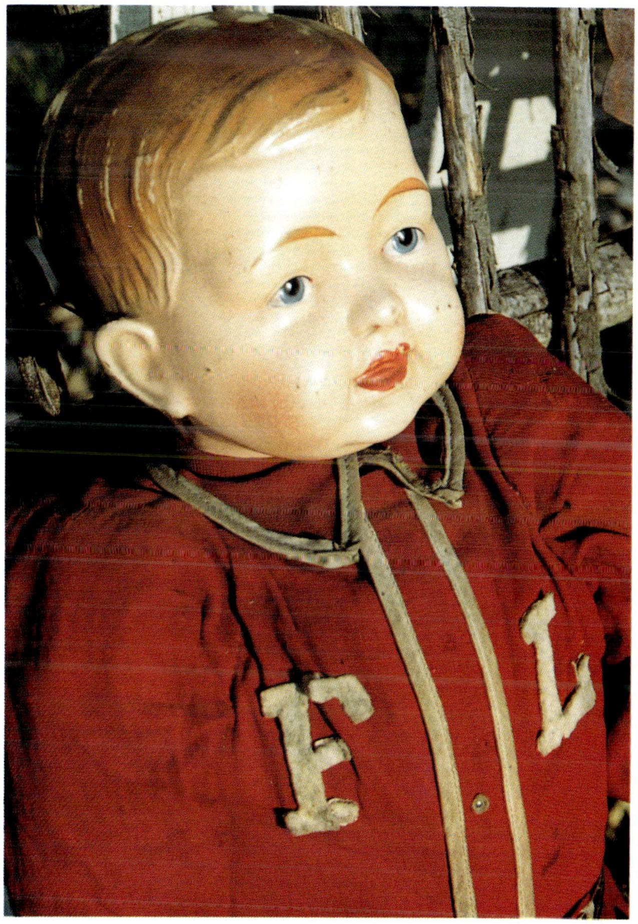

This doll in a baseball uniform was found in the attic of a home under demolition in Utica, New York. The doll was created to celebrate the opening of the Federal League season in Buffalo, New York on May 11, 1914 when the Baltimore Terrapins played the Buffeds. $3000–4000

B18 Blankets—The 1914 Cloth Baseball Cards

by Lou Hagenbruch

Until a fall morning in 1981, I had only seen pictures of the 1914 Blankets. That Monday morning a teaching colleague, who was also a serious antique collector, walked into my classroom and dropped 19 of the blankets (only one duplicate) on my desk. They had been in the top drawer of a chest-of-drawers, and were thrown in with its purchase. At the time they had little value, but I knew they were worth something. Chuck did not want anything for them, since he had paid nothing for them.

The blankets were 5 ¼" felt squares with a colorful baseball image on them. These pieces of baseball memorabilia were folded and attached to packs of cigarettes. It is thought that they came with packs of a number of cigarette brand names. However, the only complete packages discovered thus far are of one brand, Egyptienne Straight Cigarettes. Occasionally, pieces of the wrapping material can still be found attached to the back sides of some felts. Only 10 of the then 16 major league teams are represented in the set. Each team comes in two different color combinations, and each team has nine players represented. So, there were supposed to be 180 blankets in the entire set.

On a blanket is a centered player, either standing or in an action pose, with name below and flanked on each side by a pennant containing the city on the left, and league initials on the right. This is all surrounded by a square (diamond) representing basepaths, and in each corner is a small square for bases with baseball articles contained within: home (crossed bats), 1st base (baseball), 2nd base (catcher's mask) and 3rd base (fielder's glove). It appears that each blanket started as an all-white piece of felt which was imprinted with dark brown or black images, followed by the various colors. All the felts are outlines in dark brown and contain two or three other colors dependent up on whether or not white is part of the color scheme. The variety in the set comes about through the coloration of four areas: bases, basepaths, infield, and pennants. However, the pennants are the color of either the bases or basepaths.

With only 9 players per team, that means 16 were omitted. As already mentioned, only 10 out of 16 teams were included. Many future Hall of Famers were left out of the felt set. How the teams and players were chosen is anybody's guess. Along with Joe Jackson, the following Hall of Fame players were among the blankets: Maranville, Stengel, Wheat, Cobb, Chance, Carey, Wallace, Huggins, and Walter Johnson. Some names of players picked were misspelled. The ten teams included were the Boston Braves, Brooklyn Dodgers, New York Giants, Pittsburgh Pirates, and St. Louis Cardinals for the National League and the Cleveland Indians, Detroit Tigers, New York Yankees, St. Louis Browns, and Washington Senators for the American League.

The value of the individual blankets in the set ranges widely. What is the condition of the edges—straight, evenly balanced on all sides as opposed to crooked, frayed or full of needle marks (blankets were sometimes sewn together for pillows or quilts). How are the colors—clear, even, and sharp versus bled, faded, or overlapped? How rare is the particular color combination or player blanket? Is the player noteworthy or a member of the Hall of Fame? These are all factors the collector must consider in determining value or before purchasing a blanket. The monetary worth of the felts has escalated greatly in the last 15 to 20 years. What used to sell for $2 or $3, now sells for $15 to $25, and those bringing $25 to $35, now command $400 to $600. A rare, red infield Ty Cobb blanket with a suspected printing error can bring as much as $10,000.

Few dealers at sports collectors conventions have the blankets anymore, but it is not unusual to find one or two dealers at a large show with some in their booths. Sometimes felts are found for sale or part of auction listings in various collectors' publications. Last, but certainly not least, it is still possible to come across an occasional blanket at a flea market or garage sale. It would be close to impossible to amass a complete set today. However, it is well within the realm of possibilities to acquire all nine players from a single team or one of each color combination, less a rare, red felt. I had a head start and have been able to do both with less expensive blankets during the last 15 years. Even one or two felts are a nice addition to anyone's baseball card or memorabilia collection.

Notes on Collecting 1914 Felt Blankets

1. First issued in 1914 with several different cigarette brands as a premium.
2. The 5¼" per side felt blankets were taped or otherwise fastened to the pack of cigarettes. Fold marks may still show.
3. Uncut sheets of felt blankets are occasionally found.
4. Many of the blankets were eventually sewn together as pillow covers or blankets.
5. Red infields are especially rare. Most that have been found are on blankets that depict players from the Dodgers or Tigers.
6. Value is largely a function of the player's celebrity.
7. The single most desirable felt blanket would be Ty Cobb with a red infield.
8. Condition is critical to the value and collectors should be selective. To attempt to build a full set with all the variations is a serious undertaking.
9. The following members of the Hall of Fame have felt blankets:
Maranville, Stengel, Wheat, Cobb, Chance, Carey, Wallace, Huggins, and Walter Johnson.
10. There is not a huge demand for 1914 felt blankets because most baseball memorabilia collectors are oblivious to the players in the set other than the 9 Hall of Famers. As is the case with most collectibles, the individuals who are interested take it very seriously.

Ty Cobb. $550

Max Carey. $90

"Rabbit" Maranville. $80

Joe Jackson. $850

James "Red" Smith. $25

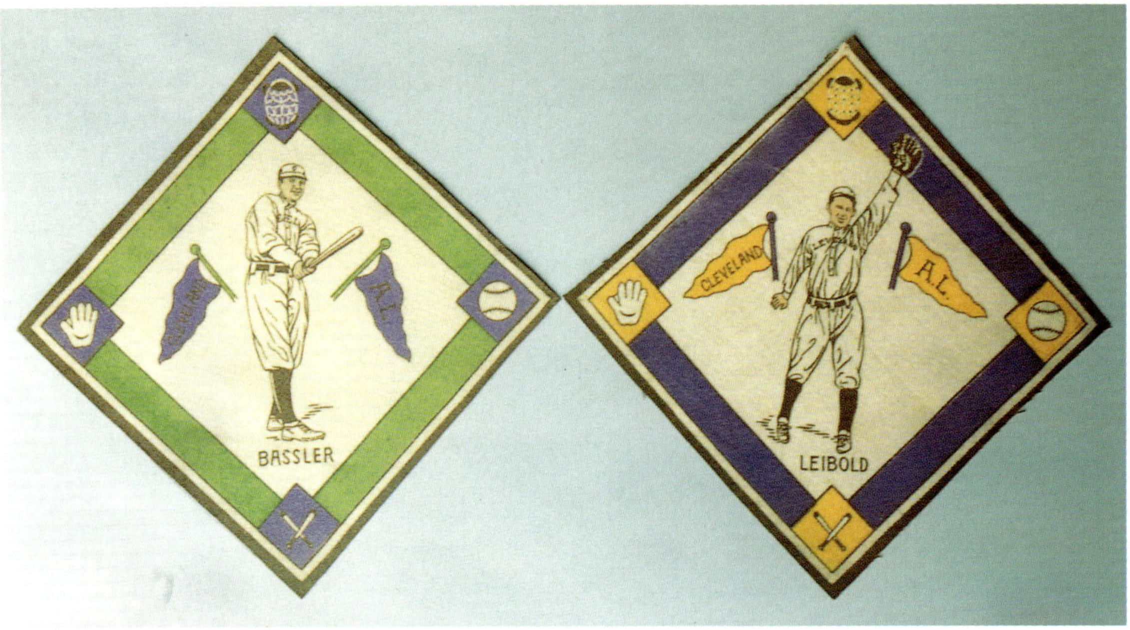

John Bassler and Nemo Leibold. $45 and $90

Zack Wheat. $100

Frank Chance. $75

Bobby Wallace. $100

Marty Kavanaugh (Kavanagh) is representative of several of the blankets with misspelled names. Kavanagh played with Detroit, Cleveland, and the Cardinals, from 1914 to 1918 when his major league career concluded. He died in 1960.

This blanket still carries some of the adhesive used to hold it to the package of cigarettes and the original creases from being folded.

Ray Morgan. $25 (each)

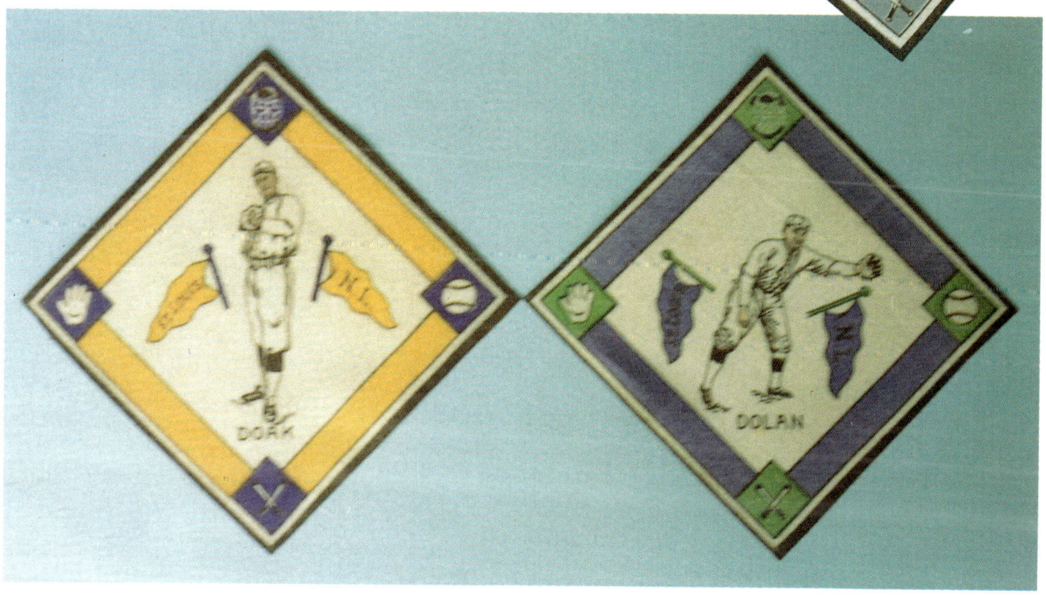

Bill Doak, $35. Cozy Dolan, $45.

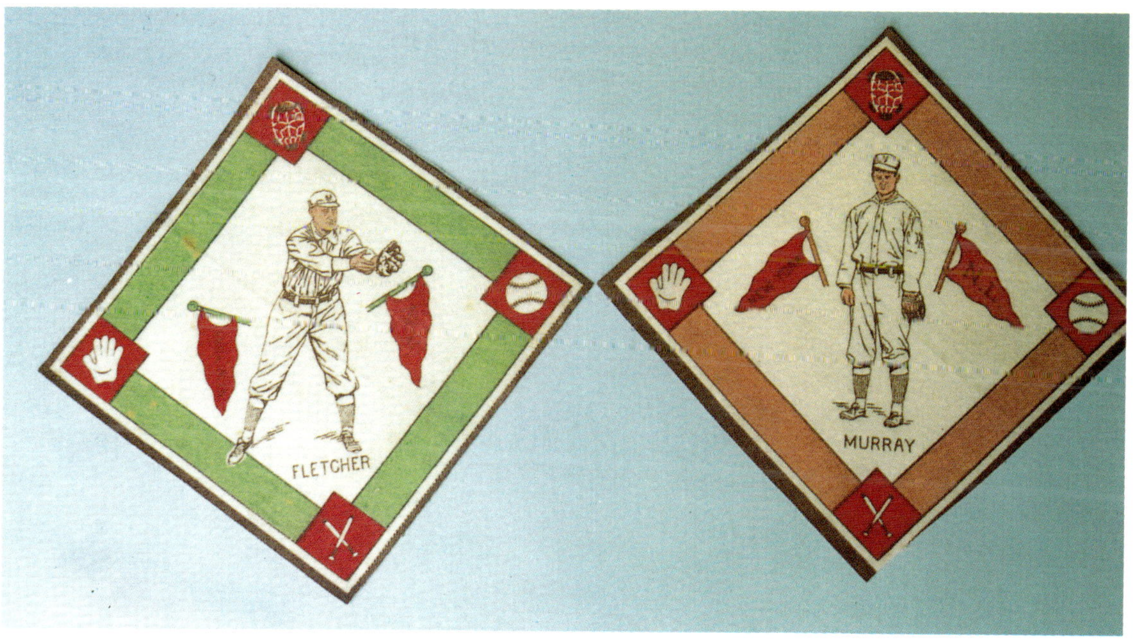

Art Fletcher, $25. Red Murray, $25.

The Ethan Allen All-Star Baseball Game
(Made by Cadaco-Ellis, later Cadaco)

by Loren Logsdon

Looking back from a perspective of almost fifty years, I can see clearly that Christmas of 1948 was the most memorable and influential one in my life, for underneath the tree was a present that has given me much pleasure and excitement over the years. When I unwrapped the present, I discovered that it was the 1948 edition of Ethan Allen's All-Star Baseball Game which my mother had ordered from the Sears-Roebuck catalog. I fell totally in love with the game; it was a classic case of love at first sight and somewhat akin to the boy and his dog syndrome. The All-Star Baseball Game coincided neatly with the intense interest I had developed in major league baseball as the result of following Harry Caray's broadcasts of the St. Louis Cardinal games over the radio. The combination of Harry Caray and Ethan Allen's All-Star Baseball Game worked to cast a spell of enchantment over me which has endured my entire life and given me many fascinating hours of enjoyment. I was so enthralled by baseball in my youth that I can say in truth that I was never bored. When I tell people that, they look at me as if I were abnormal or lying to them. To be completely honest, I became a fanatic in my devotion to the game, so much so that even earning a doctorate in English and teaching in college for thirty-six years did not cause me to outgrow the game.

To a normal person or a casual observer, there seems little about the game itself that would inspire such devotion. The regular edition of the 1948 Ethan Allen All-Star Baseball game came in a cardboard box that was twenty-two inches long, twelve inches wide, and one and one-half inches deep. It featured a playing board with a spinner and a miniature baseball diamond with the key to the game at the upper part of the playing board where the outfield would be. There were forty-two circular cardboard discs—two strategy discs and forty player discs containing the numbers 1 through 14. The players were actually the names of real major league players, and each player's name was printed at the top of the disc with the position he played at the bottom. The numbers on the disc were in proportion to the player's actual performance as determined by the kinds of outs, the kinds of hits, and the number of walks. The game promised that the player discs would perform about the same way that the players did in the actual season, and that promise was rather accurate except for the pitching. In the Ethan Allen game there was no way to reflect pitching strength, and the pitcher made the difference in the game only if he was a good hitter, unless, of course, if one had strong faith in a particular pitcher. The inside of the game box explained how teams were to be chosen, and the games were played by the rules and procedures of real baseball. Each manager would make up a lineup and spin each player disc as a time at bat. The spin would determine what had happened. The game came with four wooden pegs to use for the batter and the base runners and a small supply of scorecards. But after a while you didn't need the pegs, and you found that the scorecards were not adequate to record individual performances. Most of us quit using the pegs after we had memorized the number key, and most of us developed our own scorecard and way of keeping score so that we would have an accurate record of statistics.

I met Ethan Allen in 1975, and I discovered that he didn't realize what a great game he had invented. He thought it was a simple game for kids and did not anticipate that it would appeal as much to adults as to kids. Why was Ethan Allen's All-Star Baseball Game so great? Why did I not forsake it when I put aside other childish toys? There are essentially three reasons that I would offer as answers, but they still might not convince a non-believer. First, you have to love baseball; that is a fundamental and necessary requirement. That means that you have to love the game and understand its potential purity. You have to ignore the greed of the current players and owners and the corruption that threatens the game. In fact, All-Star Baseball does away with the criminal activity and trashy behavior that seem so prevalent among the current players. You have to understand the possibility for heroic action that is always there in baseball in spite of the very flawed human beings who play the game. In All-Star Baseball, the players are always on their best behavior and trying to do their best. Second, you have to be interested in statistics because every action in a major league baseball game is potentially a statistic. As Steve Tietz, one of my favorite All-Star Baseball friends, is fond of saying, "Major League baseball and the Ethan Allen All-Star Baseball game are the only places in life where numbers fascinate me." The statistical accuracy of Ethan Allen's game (except for pitching) gives it a strong appeal. The game offers you the chance to manage Babe Ruth and see if his disc can hit sixty or more homers in a season. Third, you have to have a high degree of imagination. To the casual observer or non-fanatic, you put a player's disc on the spinner, give the spinner a spin, and the spinner lands on number 1 (which is a homerun). "So what's the big deal?" asks the casual observer. But to a dedicated player of the game, something magical happens. You actually visualize the ball soaring over the outfield wall. Another good friend was fond of saying, "That baby is gone!" every time he would spin a homerun. He could see the ball leaving the park because he loved the game so much that it stirred his imagination. It is difficult for the non-fanatic to understand what I am explaining here because many people look at the game and see only a bunch of cardboard circles, a spinner, and some wooden pegs (some people believe that the pegs are the most important part of the game). But as New York Mets pitcher Tug McGraw said repeatedly throughout the 1969 season, "You gotta believe!"

During my youth, I usually played All-Star Baseball by myself instead of against an opponent, and the game was fun to play alone. Today, I like to think that playing the game by myself caused me to develop a strong sense of honesty and fairness because I forced myself not to show any favoritism on the close calls. As any ASB player knows, there are times when the spinner lands squarely on the line between two numbers, which means that you have to spin again. It would have been so easy to call a liner on Stan Musial a homerun instead of a liner because I had so much admiration for Stan. He represented dignity, graceful behavior, real sportsmanship, and awesome talent. I forced myself to be as objective as possible in the belief that Stan Musial would not want any unearned advantage over other players. When playing alone, I was much like the protagonist of Robert Coover's *Universal Baseball Association*, J. Henry Waugh—a fair and just god who abided by the rules and treated everyone in an even-handed manner. Indeed, I would be so audacious as to claim that fairness became a central principle in my personal code of ethics because I played so much All-Star Baseball by myself.

Until the early 1960s, I was unaware that there were others in the world as fanatic about All-Star Baseball as I was. I did share the game with Jim Holler, my best friend in high school, and I heard rumors that another kid in our high school played the game, but I never approached him about it. In 1950 I ordered a Special Edition of All-Star Baseball (40 regular players plus 40 All-time Great players), and I gave Jim my 1948 game box and duplicate players. However, Jim and I did not play the game together very often because we lived nine miles apart. When we got together, we were usually more interested in playing pitch and catch or flies and grounders instead of ASB. In 1950 I discovered that Cadaco would sell the player sets separately from the game boxes, so I ordered sets 1951 though 1955 without the game boxes. In those days Cadaco made the sets available in the early summer. I would receive a postcard from the company announcing that the new set was ready. I would send off for it, wait anxiously an eternity (it seemed) for it to arrive, and then hastily open the small box and hold those little discs of cardboard magic in my hands to see if my favorite players had been selected again or what new players had been included. I always hoped for new pitchers because the game had a notorious shortage of pitchers. Also, I was looking for players who I thought should have been included in the game but were not. For example, I could never understand why Cub slugger Hank Sauer and Cleveland catcher Jim Hegan never made the game. Years later I learned that Hegan refused to give Ethan permission to use his statistics, but I never learned why Hank Sauer had been left out. In 1981 Ethan included Hank Sauer in the 1981B edition of ASB, but that was years after Hank had retired.

From 1954 to 1958, my undergraduate college years, the game was essentially put away because I had to study so hard. In fact, the last set of player discs I purchased was 1955. Then, in 1963, when I was teaching in college, I discovered that George Hearne, another good ASB friend, had played the game as a kid and had not thrown it away. He and I decided that we would get together one night a week and play All-Star Baseball. I saw that he had sets older than 1948, and I became interested in learning about the history of the game. Consequently, I wrote to the Cadaco company and inquired about purchasing older sets. I received a note informing me that a fire had destroyed the older sets as well as many of the company records. In fact, 1959 was the oldest set available. I ordered 1959, 1960, 1961, 1962, and 1963. After that, I ordered a set from Cadaco every year until 1988, the last year that Cadaco sold the sets separately. Sets 1989, 1990, 1991, and 1993 were sold only with the game boxes. Cadaco stopped producing the game after the 1993 set because the greed of the modern baseball players made it impossible to continue to market the game.

In the early 1970s in Macomb, Illinois, I met a unique individual named Al Lindsey who had been an All-Star Baseball fanatic in his youth. Al recalled having games older than 1948; however, he did not know what year Cadaco-Ellis had first marketed the game. Al and I decided that we would form an All-Star Baseball League and try to find two other people who would join us to play a 154-game schedule. Although other managers came and went, Al and I played six full seasons, with Al winning four out of the six. We gave Al the title "The Commissioner" because of his stature, demeanor, and leadership skills. Al could be as stern as James Cagney's mother in *White Heat*, but he could also be as wise as Judge Kennesaw Mountain Landis. I don't intend to suggest that Commissioner Lindsey was meaner than nine miles of bad road; quite the contrary, he was a person of considerable wit, charm, and compassion. But he used psychological tactics in the game to combine with his baseball genius to make him the most formidable All-Star Baseball player I have ever known. Many times I have sat helplessly watching as Al would rally with two outs and no one on base in the bottom of the ninth inning to beat me, making me feel as useless as Patty Duke's father on the *Patty Duke Show*.

My friendship with Al Lindsey inspired me to renew my efforts to learn about the game because Al maintained that in his youth he had played with certain ASB players that none of us could find in our collections. To this very day, Al swears that he played with Johnny Vander Meer, Rudy York, and Johnny Lindell—players who do not appear in any of the Cadaco games of the early era. Once again I wrote to Cadaco, but this time Doug Bolton, President of Cadaco, answered my letter, repeating the earlier information about the records being destroyed by a fire. However, Mr. Bolton did something that raised my interest in All-Star Baseball to a higher level: He sent me the names and addresses of other people who had written about the game. Thus I was able to write to Skip Sesling, Karl Klukas, Mike Garrett, Larry Kilbride, Joe Owens, and John Rose. It was indeed a miracle to discover that there were other fanatics out there who were as passionate about All-Star Baseball as I was.

The recognized leader of this group of wonderful people was John Rose of Virginia, who started a newsletter which, beyond a couple years of silence, is still being produced today. Although friendly, generous, and kind, John Rose has the staying power of a pit bull when it comes to promoting All-Star Baseball. Because of his energy and leadership, we know a great deal about the history of the game. John communicated extensively with Ethan Allen and Doug Bolton to try to track things down, and his efforts resulted in an All-Star Baseball Convention in Chicago in 1975. The weekend events included a tour of Cadaco, the opportunity to meet and visit with Ethan Allen, an All-Star Baseball tournament, and a Cubs game at Wrigley Field. But the highlight of the weekend was Ethan Allen himself, who seemed a bit bewildered by the variety of people who had come. Although warm and gracious to everyone, Ethan seemed at times to be as disappointed as Dr. Frankenstein when his monster finally came to life.

Indeed, the group was highly diverse, including a couple of pre-teens, a good number of teenagers, several young adults, some middle-aged athletes, and even some elderly folk—all brought together by their love of the game. There were highly successful people in attendance—in business, in college teaching, in counseling, and in other walks of life as well. When Ethan addressed the group at the Saturday breakfast, he peered at us in disbelief and told us that he thought he was inventing a game for kids. Clearly, he had not anticipated that the game would continue to interest us as adults.

Ethan Allen explained how he had invented the game and especially how he had to obtain legal written permission from the players in order to use their statistics in the game. He told us that most players signed readily but that some caused him problems. He mentioned that Hal Newhouser had at first declined but later had signed and that Jim Hegan had refused to sign and could not be persuaded to change his mind. But the saddest case of all involved a premier relief pitcher whom I will not name. The pitcher was indeed a star and deserved to be included in the game. In an effort to convince him to sign, Ethan mailed him a sample All-Star Baseball Game. To Ethan's dismay, the pitcher sent him a crisp note telling Ethan not to clutter his mailbox with any more garbage. If only that pitcher had known that what he had called garbage was a priceless treasure to many others, but then it just goes to show that some people in this world have the imagination of a fence post and the sensitivity of a three-day-old dead toad.

One of John Rose's early projects in the newsletter was to coordinate our efforts and develop accurate player lists for each year that the game was produced. He hoped that Ethan Allen could clear up most of the uncertainty about the lists, but Ethan's own records were not complete, so he could not provide the absolute authority that we needed. Ethan did remember that he had tried to persuade several toy companies to market the game and that all his efforts had failed until he approached Donald Mazer of Cadaco-Ellis. Ethan thought that 1941 was the first year that the game was produced, and fans have found a few of those games although the 1941 game is considered to be rare. The 1942 game was produced and sold with the same players in 1943 and 1944. The next known game is 1946, which leaves 1945 unaccounted for. Was there a 1945 game? We have developed complete player lists from 1941 to 1944 and from 1946 to 1993 (no game was produced in 1992). The player lists for those years can be verified for accuracy. However, no one has ever found a 1945 game or a 1945 set of players or even a stray player or two that would indicate the existence of a 1945 game. Some ASB people believe that the 1942 set was also issued in 1945 and that there was no 1945 set as such. What makes others think that a 1945 game was produced is the testimony of Al Lindsey and, years later, a conversation I had with Ron Greek, the Associate Dean and Registrar at Eureka College. Ron recalls seeing the discs for Johnny Vander Meer and Snuffy Stirnweiss. Ron did not have those players in a game of his own, but he does recall seeing an older youth in his neighborhood use those two players. Since Vander Meer and Stirnweiss, like Hank Sauer, were not included on any player list until Ethan Allen's 1981B and 1983B games, it is possible that a 1945 game exists that no one has found or identified correctly.

From the mid-1970s to the present, we have been searching for the 1945 game. I have searched in antique malls and flea markets throughout the Midwest. I have had antique dealers tell me that they have seen the game in a mall fifty miles to the west, and I have come to know what the Spanish explorers must have felt when the Indians would tell them that the Seven Cities of Cibola were just beyond the next mountain. Good friends such as Don Raycraft, Jim Holler, George Hearne, Ron Greek, Bruce Hilk, Les O'Neal, and Dee Thomas have found games for me. I have asked flea market dealers to watch out for games for me, but the 1945 game has not turned up. The fact that no one has found the game does not necessarily mean that it does not exist. Some of the games that we do know exist are difficult to find. For example, in all of my searching I have never found a 1946 or a 1941 game, and I have found only one 1947 game and one 1953 game. By contrast, some of the games are easy to find. I have found eight 1955 games, five 1961 games, and so many 1988 games that I have lost count.

In 1995 John Rose published a monumental issue of the All-Star Baseball News in which he included player lists for all of the known Ethan Allen All-Star Baseball games. In that same issue he has an alphabetical list of individual players and the year of each set in which they appeared. For example, Stan Musial appears in seventeen different sets. That means that there are seventeen different discs of Stan Musial and that no two discs are exactly the same. For the serious collectors of the game, John Rose's player list is essential for purposes of identification.

Those of you who are starting out to collect All-Star Baseball games will quickly discover that there are serious problems of identification. For one thing, the game boxes prior to 1968 have three different years listed. One year will be found on the outside of the box, another on the inside of the box lid, and another on the playing field or the scoreboard. The early games had a player list on the inside of the box lid, but that practice was discontinued after 1952. So the specific game cannot always be identified by the year or years that appear on the game box. From 1941 through 1954 the regular editions came in a blue box, but one person found the 1954 game in a green box. The only reliable way of identifying is by the player lists which are published in the 1995 October issue of All-Star Baseball News.

From 1946 through 1954 Cadaco-Ellis produced a Special Edition of All-Star Baseball. The game box is slightly longer than the regular edition, and there are more player discs. The inside of the box lid of the Special Edition lists the players for that edition. From 1946 through 1948 the game box is blue, the same as the regular edition. From 1950 through 1954 the game box is red.

From 1955 through 1967 Cadaco issued only the regular edition which also contains a set of All Time Great players. That practice ended with the 1968 game, which contains only the current players. If you find a game with the year 1968 on the box lid, that game could be anything from 1968 to 1988, and the player list is the only way of certain identification of a specific year.

In 1975 Cadaco issued a first set that had only eight numbers on the discs instead of the usual 14. There was such an outcry of complaint from the fans that the company had to issue a revised set containing the customary 14 numbers. Apparently the change to eight numbers was some kind of an experiment, but it was not accepted by the All-Star Baseball fans. Because we complained so vehemently, the experiment was as doomed as a woman who found herself engaged to one of *Bonanza's* Cartwright sons. Historically, this ill-advised experiment by Cadaco gave ASB fans their own unique insult comparable to flipping someone the bird. After 1975, if you wanted to insult an ASB fanatic, all you had to do was to point a gnarled spinner finger at him and say, "May your disc have only eight numbers and your spinner always land squarely on the line."

There are some special things for collectors to watch for. In 1952, Cadaco issued two sets, an A and a B set. The B set is hard to find, and we are not sure that it was issued widely in a game box. Again, though, a player list is the most reliable way of identifying the set. Cadaco issued A and B sets in the following years: 1970, 1976, 1977, 1978, 1979, and 1980. In the aforementioned years, both the A and B sets came in game boxes. In 1980 Ethan Allen produced a special Cadaco Hall of Fame Game, featuring many players who were in the Baseball Hall of Fame but also several players who were not yet so honored. The Hall of Fame Game came in a green box with an electric spinner, making it easy to identify.

From 1981 through 1985 Cadaco offered A and B sets; however, the B set did not come in a game box. In 1989 the game box was changed quite drastically to the shape of the 1980 Hall of Fame Game, but the color was red instead of green. This style was used from 1989 through 1993. There was a major change in the player discs: the player's picture appeared on the discs and the statistics on the back of the disc much like a Topps baseball card. Thus from 1941 through 1993 the Cadaco company marketed at least one game per year except for 1945 and 1992. We are certain that no game was issued in 1992, but some of us are still looking for the 1945 game.

There are other special All-Star Baseball items to look for. Sometime in the late 1960s or early 1970s Cadaco issued special sets of twenty players per set. The players on these sets were stars and superstars from the 1950s and the 1960s. Some of the players were retired and some were in the twilight of their career. These sets are numbered #1 through #10 and listed in the All-Star Baseball News. Then sometime later sets #1, #4, #5, #7, and #9 were revised. These sets are rare because they did not come with a game box; they had to be ordered directly from the company. There was a Travel Edition of the game issued in 1990.

In addition, there were mistakes and corrections in the game over the years, such as the incorrect spelling of a player's name and the wrong position printed on the disc. The 1969 game is full of errors in player position and had to be corrected. For example, John Bateman is listed as a pitcher instead of a catcher. A revised set was issued to correct the errors. In fact, John Rose has discovered at least three variations of the 1969 game.

To any collectors who seek a complete collection of the games as well as the errors and variations, you really need to obtain a copy of All-Star Baseball News, No. 49 (October 1995). In the near future John Rose is planning to revise the player list to include some of the variations he has discovered after the 1995 list was published.

The Ethan Allen All-Star Baseball Game has flourished from 1941 to 1993. Its popularity has shown no respect for the "generation gap" that has divided people in the last half of the twentieth century. I am amazed at the number of people who have told me that they played the game in their youth. Obviously some of us still enjoy the game. It has been a pleasurable hobby and an exciting escape from the harsh realities of the real world. The game has endured so long because of the dedication of its creator, Ethan Allen, who was tireless in his pursuit of major league baseball players to give him permission to use their names and their statistics. However, since the early 1970s the game has been faithfully supported by John Rose's newsletter, which has, through the efforts of Larry Kilbride and Ken Thompson, introduced changes and refinements to improve the pitching aspect of the game so that pitching is now important. In addition, the base-stealing factor has been refined to make the game more realistic than it was before 1970. These two refinements in no way destroy the wonderful simplicity of Ethan Allen's game; rather, they serve to make the game more fascinating and enjoyable for those of us young or old—who love baseball.

If you have any questions about Ethan Allen's All-Star Baseball Game, if you have All-Star Baseball Games you want to sell, or if you want advice about buying games, please call or write to either of the people listed below. If you are interested in the All-Star Baseball News, its headquarters are at John Rose's address.

Loren Logsdon
1014 Redbud Lane
Eureka, IL 61530
Phone: (309) 467-3311

John Rose
5904 Mount Eagle Drive #1610
Alexandria, VA 22303
Phone: (703) 329-0274

Notes on the Price Guide

The Ethan Allen All-Star Baseball Games can be roughly categorized in terms of the following five eras, and a collector can generally place a game in an era by the color of the game box, the discs, and the spinner.

Eras:

Blue Box 1941–1954 Discs with center cut out. Regular spinner
Green Box 1955–1962
Action Boxes 1962–1968
Photo Box 1969–1988 Centers not cut out of discs. Plastic sleeve with spinner
Red Box with Discs on cover 1989–1993

Completeness and condition are very important in pricing the games. If there are player discs missing or if the discs are worn, bent, or written on, then these factors severely decrease the values listed in the price guide. The condition of the box, the playing board, and the scoreboard are also important. In addition, there should be four pegs (wooden for the early games and plastic for the later ones), scoresheets, and AD and FJ strategy discs for the game to be considered complete. The value in the price guide is base on the game being in excellent condition, but prices should be adjusted according to the condition of the game.

LIKE NEW: The game has never been played and is complete. For early editions the discs may have a tan look. For later editions—after 1958—the discs should not have been punched out of the light sheets of cardboard they came in. If the game is in this condition, add 20% to the value listed in the price guide.

EXCELLENT: The disc should show no wear. The box may have scratches and a split corner, but there should be no tape. The game should be complete. The price for a game in this condition will be the one listed in the price guide.

VERY GOOD: The condition is basically the same as excellent except that more than one corner may be split. There may be tape on the box and the playing board may show same wear. The discs may have minor wear, and the pegs and scoresheets may be missing. Deduct 20% from the price guide if the game is in this condition.

GOOD: Generally there is more wear on the box than the condition above. The discs may be worn from heavy use, and the spinner may be in bad condition. Maybe one or two discs are missing. Deduct 40% from the price guide if the game is in this condition.

POOR: There are several discs missing and the ones in the game are badly worn or damaged. The box has missing tabs or other damage, and the playing board has significant damage or wear. The spinner may be bent, broken, or missing. For a game in this condition, deduct 60% from the price guide.

Year	Date	Player	Value
1941	1941	Clift	$150
1942/5	1942	Sisti	$40
1946	1946	Hal Gregg	$75
1947	1946	Emil Verban	$75
1948	1946	Spec Shea	$65
1949	1949	Gene Bearden	$65
1950	1950	None	$60
1951	1951	Gerry Coleman	$55
1952A	1952	Gil Coan	$60
1952B	1953	Matt Batts	$90
1953	1953	Joe Black	$65
1954	1953	Jim Delsing	$65
1955	1954	Virgil Trucks	$50
1956	1954	Wally Post	$60
1957	1957	John Kucks	$50
1958	1957	Ted Lepcio	$50
1959	1957	Bob Boyd	$40
1960	1959	Sam Taylor	$40
1961	1959	Bud Daley	$40
1962	1959	Andy Carey	$40
1963	1962	Joey Jay	$60
1964	1962	Ken Hubbs	$40
1965	1962	Bernie Allen	$40
1966	1962	Walt Bond	$40
1967	1966	Wally Bunker	$50
1968	1966	Phil Regan	$40
1969	1966	None	$40
1970A	1968	Jim Nash	$35
1970B	1968	Russ Snyder	$55
1971	1968	Jim Hickman	$35
1972	1968	Manny Mota	$35
1973	1968	Duffy Dyer	$35
1974	1968	John Briggs	$35
1975	1968	Pat Kelly	$10
1975C	1968	Pat Kelly	$50
1976A	1968	Von Joshua	$30
1976B	1968	John Hiller	$40
1977A	1968	Mark Fidrych	$30
1977B	1968	Rick Rhoden	$40
1978A	1968	Bill North	$30
1978B	1968	Doug Ault	$40
1979A	1968	None	$25
1979B	1968	Ray Burris	$35
1980A	1968	Rusty Stuab	$20
1980B	1968	Pat Putnam	$35
1980H	1979	Ethan Allen	$65
1981A	1968	None	$20
1981B	1968	Joe Jackson	$30
1982A	1968	Ron Oester	$20
1982B		Jim Busby	$35
1983A	1968	None	$20
1983B		Steve Yeager	$35
1984A	1968	Eddie Stanky	$20
1984B		Dale Berra	$35
1985A	1968	Dickie Thon	$20
1985B		Storm Davis	$35
1986	1968	Lamar Hoyt	$15
1987	1968	Alvin Davis	$15
1988	1968	Rob Deer	$10
1989	1989	Juan Samuel	$10
1990	1989	Rob Thompson	$15
1990T1	1990	None	$15
1990T2	1990	None	$15
1991	1989	Barry Bonds	$15
1993	1989	Frank Thomas	$15

Date is the date on the inside of the box top.

Player is unique to that year. For example, Clift was only in 1941.

Special Editions were issued from 1946 through 1954. Add 50% to the value of the regular edition.

Helpful Suggestions

You will find very few games in the LIKE NEW category, so most of the games you will buy or sell will be in the EXCELLENT to POOR category. I have a 1947 game and a 1961 game that are LIKE NEW, but those are the only ones I have in that condition.

How to use the price guide: Since I have found eight 1955 games, and they have ranged in condition for EXCELLENT to POOR, I will use 1955 as an example. If you find a 1955 game in LIKE NEW condition, you would add 20% to $50.00 and pay $60.00 for the game. If you find one in EXCELLENT condition, you would pay the $50.00 price that is listed in the guide. In VERY GOOD condition, you would pay $40.00; in GOOD condition $30.00; and in POOR condition $20.00. A 1955 game with almost all of the discs missing and in bad condition is worth maybe $5.00 if you need the box, but as a game it would not be worth much to the serious collector.

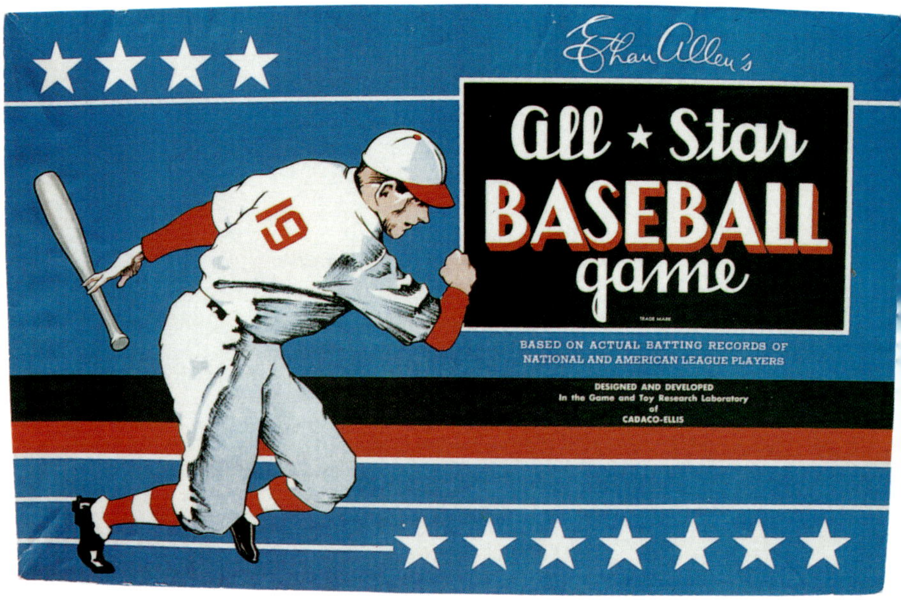

Box used between 1941 and 1954.

All-Star Baseball box used in 1962.

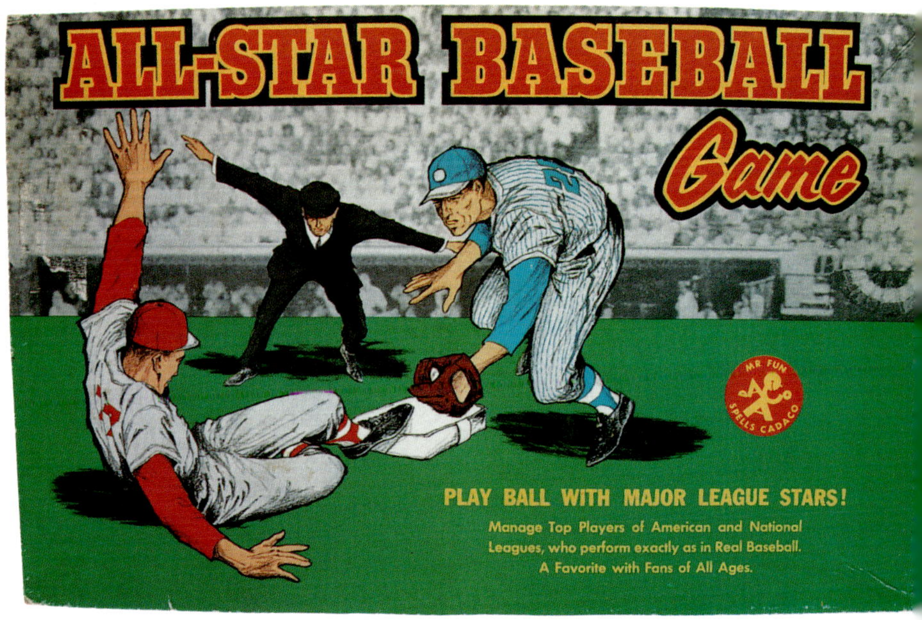

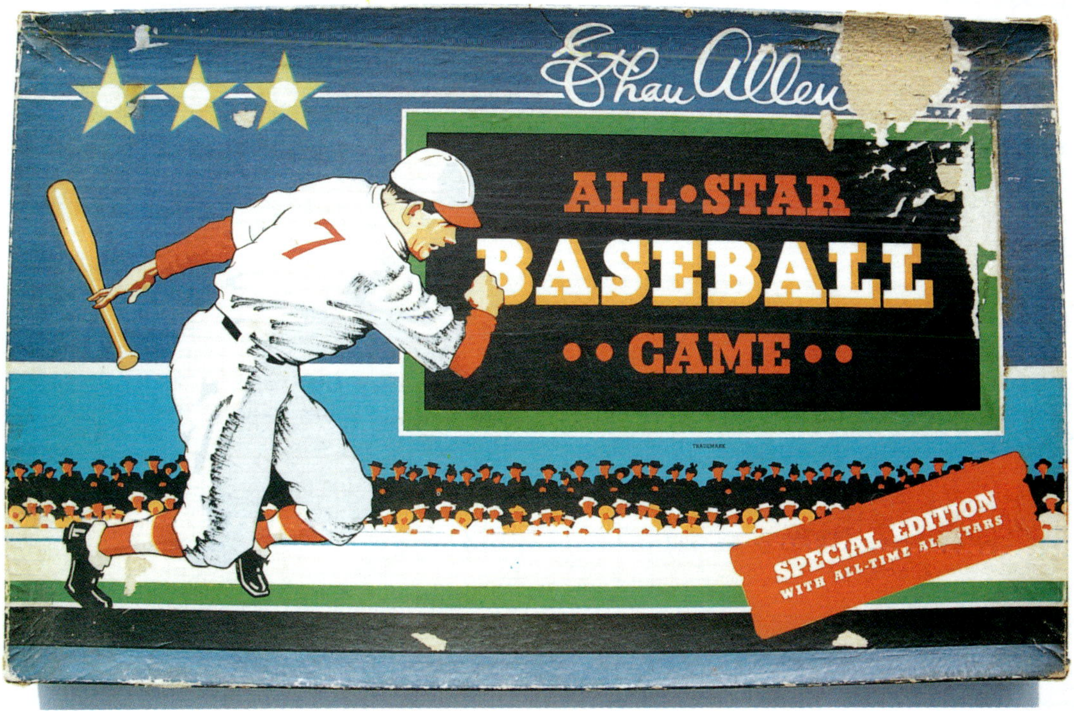

Special Edition box used between 1946and 1949.

All-Star Baseball box used between 1954–1962.

All-Star Baseball box used between 1963–1966.

All-Star Baseball box used between 1966–1969.

All-Star Travel box used in 1990.

All-Star Baseball box used between 1977–1988.

All-Star Baseball Box from 1974.

All-Star Baseball game Hall of Fame edition box from 1980.

Joe Tinker disc from the Hall of Fame edition.

Game board from 1980 Hall of Fame edition.

All-Star Baseball game box used between 1989 and 1993.

1941 brochure advertising other Cadaco Ellis games from All-Star Baseball box.

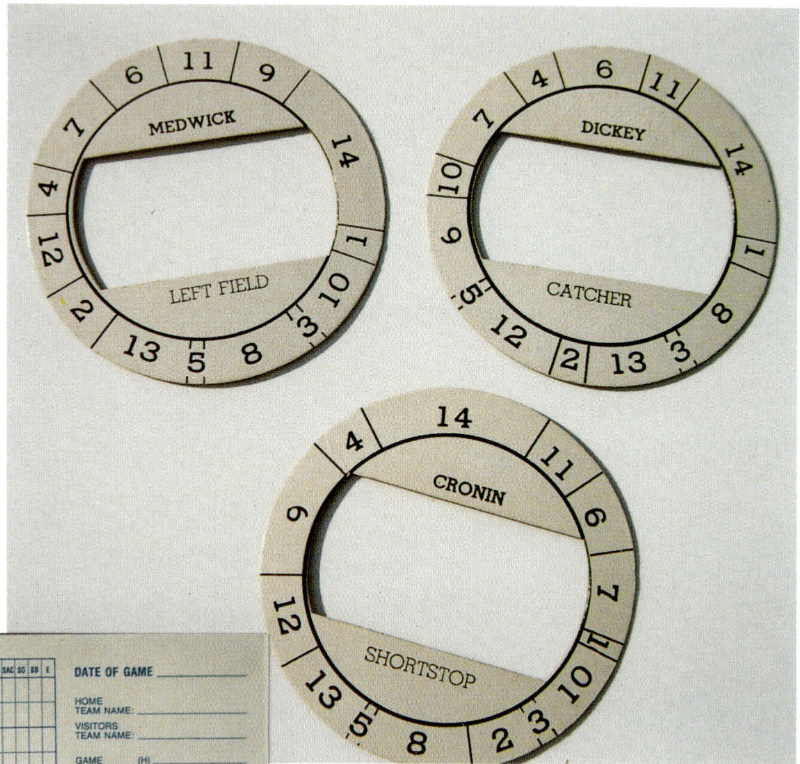

1941 discs of Cronin, Dickey, and Medwick.

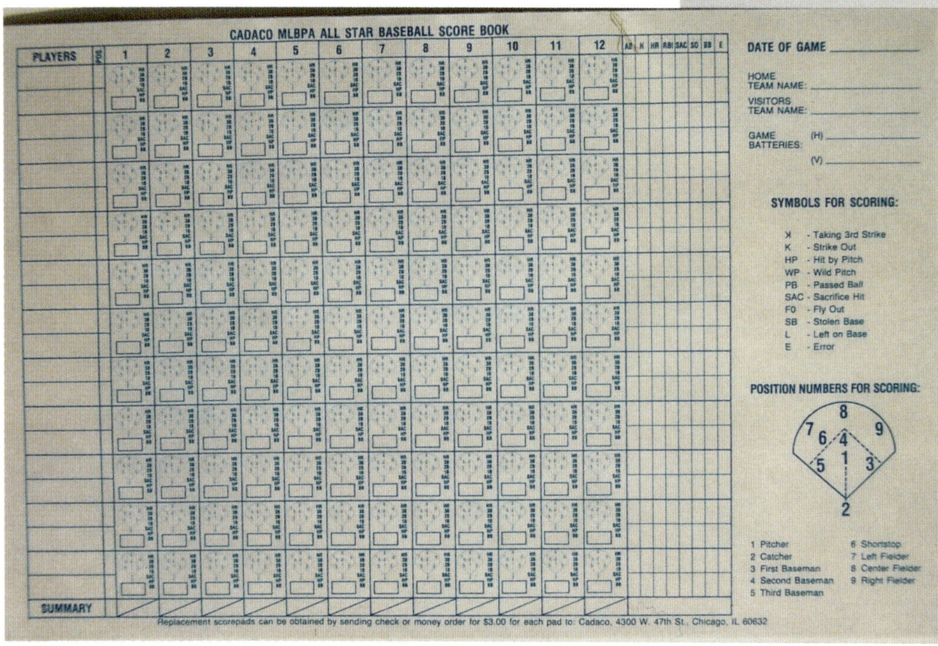

1989–93 scoring sheet from All-Star Baseball.

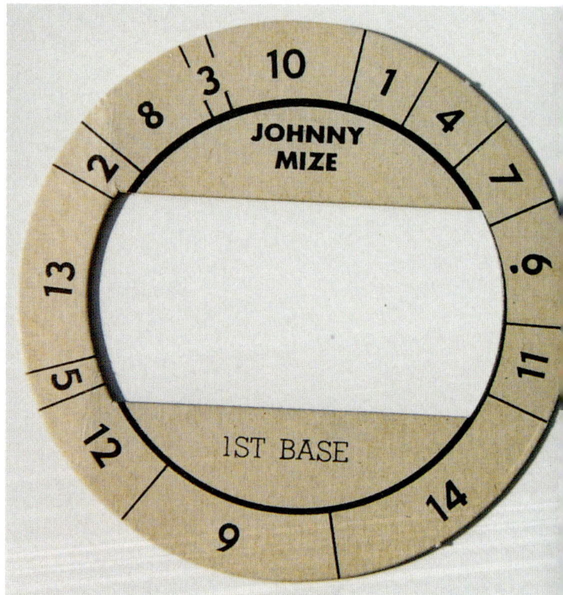

Johnny Mize disc from 1947.

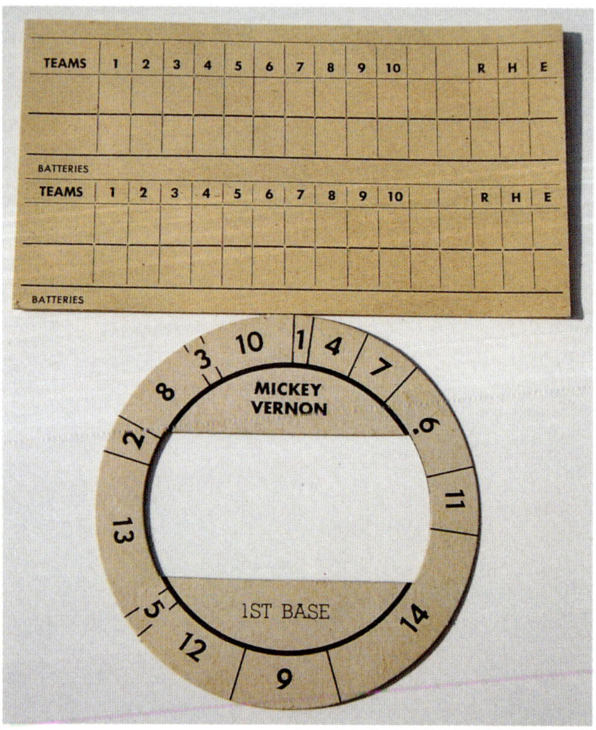

1940s scoring sheet and 1947 Mickey Vernon disc. The slim "1" area of Vernon's disc indicates he was a minimal homerun threat.

Chapter 5

Cooperstown

Cooperstown hasn't always been in love with ball. Long before Albert Spalding and his quest for answers, the Cooperstown board of trustees in 1816 passed an ordinance that had a major effect on early ball in the community. The ordinance decreed "Be it ordained that no person shall play Ball in Second or West Street, in this village, under a penalty of one dollar, for each and every offence."

Why is the Hall of Fame in Cooperstown?

The National Baseball Hall of Fame is located in Cooperstown, New York because of baseball pioneer Albert Spalding; the third president of the National League, A.G. Mills; the mysterious Abner Graves; and Singer sewing machine heir Stephen Clark.

Spalding was fixated on defining baseball as an American game and not an English import. He established a group to investigate the origins of the sport and in December of 1907, the Mills Commission found that baseball was first played in Elihu Phinney's pasture (now the site of Doubleday Field) based to some extent on a letter written by Abner Graves. Graves informed the committee that he had been taught the game in Cooperstown during the summer of 1839 by Abner Doubleday. Many historians have pointed out that Doubleday was a student at West Point during the summer of 1839 and probably never made it home to Cooperstown during that period of his life. The connection between A.G. Mills and Doubleday is also interesting because Mills was a major player in the planning of Doubleday's funeral in 1893.

In 1935 Clark helped in putting together an exhibit of baseball-related material in the Cooperstown Village Club. The cornerstone of the baseball memorabilia collection was a nineteenth century baseball purchased by Mr. Clark out of an attic in the village of Fly Creek, just north of Cooperstown. Coincidentally, the trunk from which the ball emerged had belonged to the long dead Abner Graves, the childhood "friend" of Abner Doubleday.

The 100th anniversary of the "invention" of baseball in Cooperstown was approaching and Clark planned for a huge celebration in 1939. With the help of Ford Frick, William Harridge, and Kenesaw Mountain Landis, Clark saw his idea germinate into the National Baseball Hall of Fame which opened on June 12, 1939. Isolated Cooperstown soon became a mecca for baseball fanatics and a boon for local businesses.

Induction Weekend

The annual Hall of Fame Induction Weekend is held each year in Cooperstown in late July or early August. The date is dependent to some extent on the ability of major league baseball to find two teams that can be scheduled for an exhibition game on Monday at Doubleday Field.

The weekend is filled with baseball-related activities highlighted by the induction ceremony that welcomes each year's additions to the roster of the Baseball Hall of Fame.

An Insider's Guide to the Hall of Fame Weekend

Friday
- Hall of Fame members sign autographs for a fee at numerous downtown venues.

Saturday
- 500 Hall of Fame commemorative bats go on sale at the gift shop at 8 a.m.
- Hall of Fame members sign autographs for a fee at numerous downtown venues.
- Memorabilia show (15-25 dealers) across from the Hall of Fame.
- Minor league baseball game at Doubleday Field (afternoon) at no charge.
- Hall of Fame autograph signing for children (no charge).
- Auction of baseball-related memorabilia at Legion Hall across from the Hall of Fame (early evening).
- At approximately 9–9:30 p.m. there is an arrival of Hall of Fame members at the Hall for a party. Many are seen and cheered by onlookers at the entrance. Try the steps of the post office for a better view.

Sunday
- Hall of Fame members sign autographs for a fee downtown (morning and late afternoon).
- Induction Ceremony at Clark Sports Center on Lower Susquehanna Avenue (afternoon).
- Buses to the ceremony leave from and return to Doubleday Field parking lot (no charge).
- Sunday evening is an excellent time to tour the Hall of Fame.

Monday
- Annual exhibition game between two major league teams at

Doubleday Field. This game is always sold out well in advance. There are usually some tickets available from "scalpers" in front of Doubleday prior to the game. The price varies considerably as game time approaches.

- The second autograph-signing session for children (no charge) takes place in the morning at the Clark Sports Center. Information can be secured from the Hall of Fame all weekend
- Hall of Fame members sign autographs for a fee at numerous downtown sites in the morning and late afternoon.

10 Hall of Fame Weekend Tips

1. The induction ceremony is held in a large open field with minimal shade. Take a blanket, something to chew on, go early, carry sunscreen or rain gear, binoculars, and something to read. The size of the crowd is largely a function of who is going to be inducted.
2. The best time to visit the Hall of Fame is on Friday, Sunday afternoon during the induction ceremony, or Sunday evening.
3. In addition to numerous autograph signings (for a fee) up and down Main Street, there is a baseball memorabilia show in the Legion Hall.
4. For many annual visitors, it is a ritual to buy Hall of Fame plaques (postcards) of the new inductees in the gift shop of the Hall of Fame after the induction and get them postmarked at the post office (special Sunday hours) across the street.
5. The Hall of Fame does not offer the postcards of the new inductees until Sunday afternoon.
6. The Hall of Fame programs that are handed out at the induction ceremony are usually limited and are also something to get stamped and postmarked later on Sunday afternoon.
7. Do not miss the Hall of Fame gift shop for baseball-related items you will find nowhere else.
8. The bakery at Main and Chestnut (southeast corner) should be added to your list of stops along with the grill of the Tunnicliff Inn at Main and Pioneer (607-547-9611). We also suggest lunch at the Farmers' Museum just north of Cooperstown. The grilled cheese sandwich with tomato is especially appealing.
9. Parking is always a problem during induction weekend. Try finding a spot on Chestnut Street (east side) or in an "instant" parking lot that always springs up in a homeowner's yard (for a fee).
10. By joining the Friends of the Hall of Fame you receive a t-shirt, yearbook, newsletter, and a year's pass to the Hall of Fame. If you are in Cooperstown on the induction weekend, you can use your pass to enter the Hall of Fame all three days and be ahead of the game. The Hall of Fame has a website at http://www.baseballhalloffame.org.

Accommodations

Call the Cooperstown Chamber of Commerce well in advance for a brochure about motels, bed and breakfast options, and hotels. The upscale Otesaga Hotel (800-348-6222) was built in 1909 with 136 rooms, magnificent views, and an eighteen hole golf course. During Induction Weekend, the Otesaga is taken over by baseball and is closed to the general public.

The Glimmerglass State Park (eight miles north of Cooperstown on Route 31) has 36 campsites and takes reservations at 800-952-2267.

A limited number of rooms are sometimes available through Oneonta State University in nearby Oneonta, New York. Try 607-436-2079 well in advance for information.

The Cooperstown Area Guide is published by the Chamber of Commerce (607-547-9983) and lists restaurants, campgrounds, shopping, churches, and other accommodations and activities. The Chamber is located at 31 Chestnut Street, Cooperstown, N.Y. 13326. There is no charge for the guide.

How Do I Get to Cooperstown?

The community is located in central New York 30 miles south of the New York State Thruway.

From the west or north:
Exit 30 at Herkimer, south on Route 28 to Cooperstown

From east or north:
Exit 25A, I-88 to Duanesburg, west on Route 20 to Route 80, south to Cooperstown

From the south:
I-88 from Binghamton, Exit 17, Route 28 north to Cooperstown

Autographs in Cooperstown

There are typically 25-35 members of the Hall of Fame in Cooperstown each year during the Induction Weekend. A visitor to the village will probably see one of these men on the street at some point between Friday and Monday but it is unlikely an autograph will be secured. The members are usually in a hurry traveling from a signing session for pay downtown and then back to the Otesaga Hotel where they are safely ensconced.

On Saturday and Monday a large group of Hall of Fame members sign for free for children who have stood in line at the Hall of Fame. Generally there are two groupings of members and the lucky child makes a choice which "line" he/she wants to select. They are provided a specially made sheet that they can take through for the legends to sign. They also receive an autographed Hall of Fame yellow plaque from each member in their "line".

In 1995 the following members attended the children's autograph session on July 29:

Richie Ashburn	Harmon Killebrew	Pee Wee Reese
Al Barlick	Ralph Kiner	Phil Rizzuto
Yogi Berra	Bob Lemon	Brooks Robinson
Lou Brock	Juan Marichal	Robin Roberts
Bobby Doerr	Eddie Mathews	Mike Schmidt
Bob Feller	Joe Morgan	Enos Slaughter
Rollie Fingers	Stan Musial	Red Schoendienst
Monte Irvin	Hal Newhouse	Warren Spahn
George Kell	Jim Palmer	Early Wynn

Cooperstown's Hall of Fame Weekend provides a unique opportunity for promoters who want to hire baseball legends to sign autographs. They do not have to pick up lodging costs or pay for airplane tickets because the Hall of Famer is already there. The enclosed advertisement from 1995 provides some indication of the scheduling problems and procedures that face promoters and collectors in Cooperstown.

Hall of Fame outfielder and member of the 500 homerun club Frank Robinson is a frequent autograph guest during the Induction Weekend.

Legendary Negro League first baseman Buck Leonard (d. 1997) was a gracious and prolific signer of autographs during his many visits to Cooperstown after his election to the Hall of Fame in 1972.

Cardinal pitcher Bob Gibson signed hundreds of autographs during this visit to Cooperstown in 1998.

Gaylord Perry won twenty or more games five times and a Cy Young award in both the American and National Leagues. He was elected to the Hall of Fame in 1991.

Hal Newhouser was the Most Valuable Player in the American League in 1944 and 1945. He won 207 games in 17 seasons and two in the 1945 World Series. He was elected to the Hall of Fame in 1992.

Stan Musial is a baseball immortal who is a regular visitor to Cooperstown during the Induction Weekend. He was elected to the Hall of Fame in 1969 and hit over .300 eighteen times.

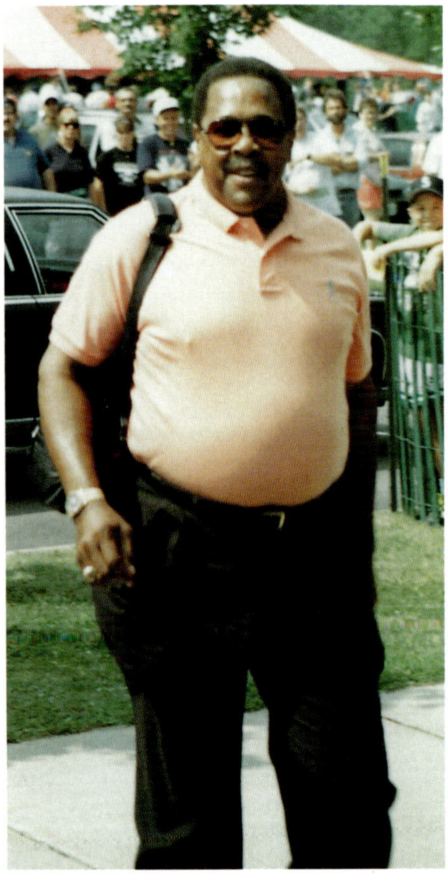

Willie Stargell hit 475 career homeruns with the Pirates and was elected to the Hall of Fame in 1988.

Bob Feller won 266 games during his career with Cleveland and lost four seasons to World War II while serving with distinction in the U.S. Navy. Feller was elected to the Hall of Fame in 1962.

Bob Lemon won 20 games seven times for the Cleveland Indians and was voted into the Hall of Fame in 1976.

Al Barlick (d. 1995) spent 27 seasons as a National League umpire and was in Cooperstown regularly after his election to the Hall of Fame in 1989.

Don Larsen had a career record of 81–91 but his perfect game in the 1956 World Series makes him a popular autograph guest in Cooperstown.

Yogi Berra was the MVP of the American League three times and was a pennant-winning manager with the Yankees and the Mets.

Cooperstown turns into autograph heaven for four days each summer during the Induction Weekend. Players sign in front of stores, in the stores, and in the basements of stores all along Main Street.

The Salvation Army holds services on Sunday morning in a small park in downtown Cooperstown. In 1998, basketball Hall of Famer David Thompson spoke and signed autographs for onlookers.

Eight Hall of Famers and former Yankee great Clete Boyer signed on Saturday of the Induction Weekend in 1998 at Mickey's Place.

Fifteen former Dodgers signed autographs at the Tunnicliff Inn in 1998.

Doubleday Field has been the site of major league exhibition games annually since 1940 with the exception of 1945 when war restrictions limited play. Rain cancelled games in 1944, 1962, 1990, and 1993. The players' strike in 1981 and a problem with an airplane in 1989 forced the Red Sox to play an intrasquad game when the Reds could not get out of Montreal. The game is always a sellout with annual crowds of about 9, 791 fans.

Mickey's Place on Main Street in Cooperstown contains a huge assortment of baseball caps and an extensive collection of Mickey Mantle memorabilia.

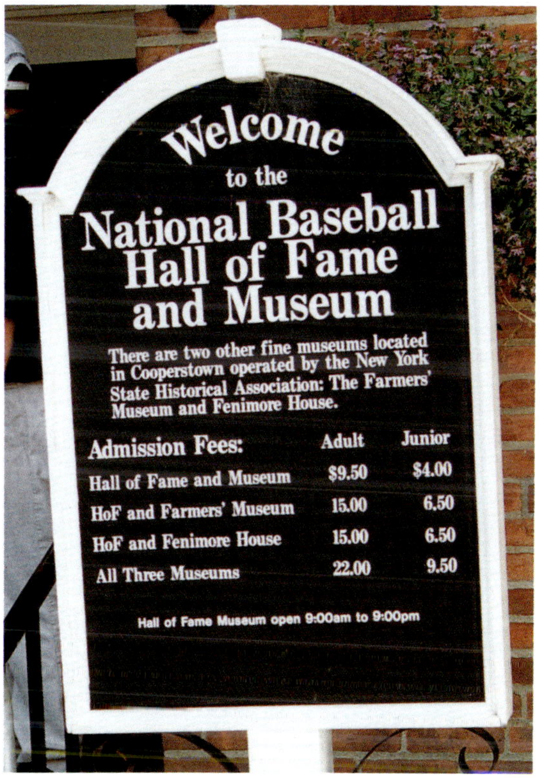

There are three major museums in Cooperstown that include the Baseball Hall of Fame, the Farmers' Museum, and Fenimore House. Combination tickets are available and are well worth the investment.

The Tunnicliff Inn is on our short list of recommended restaurants in Cooperstown.

"No Vacancy" signs are a common sight in Cooperstown during the Induction Weekend. Plans should be made months in advance.

Top left: The trolley system in Cooperstown during the summer tourist season makes moving about the village a pleasant experience when parking around the downtown area is at a premium.

Top right: It's not the Babe, because he died in 1948 and this picture was taken fifty years later, but this gentleman causes serious double takes as he walks around Cooperstown.

Center left: The memorabilia and card show held in the Legion Building each year is highlighted by a Saturday night auction.

Center right: The autograph sessions in Cooperstown in the 1980s and early 1990s gave fans from across America the opportunity to come into contact with many of their childhood heroes and develop lasting friendships while waiting in line.

Bottom right: At the 1998 Induction Weekend Larry Doby was probably the most desired autograph signer by collectors. The charge for Doby to sign a "flat" item (book, card, poster, picture) was $30.

Chapter 6

..........Putting the Pieces Together

For many baseball memorabilia collectors the primary joy is the hunt. It is the constant uncertainty and anticipation of what is out there that fuels the journey. It usually doesn't make any difference if it is the National Convention in Chicago or Atlanta or a twenty-table card show in Peoria, there is always the possibility of a major "find". Periodically there is some success—a rarity stored away several generations ago after a July trip to Yankee Stadium or Sportsman's Park floats to the surface.

Most of us want to be able to look at whatever we buy on a daily basis. Putting baseball cards in plastic sheets and storing them in a drawer just isn't enough. It is an arduous task to put the pieces of a baseball collection together in such a way that each artifact can be viewed and the memory of its acquisition savored and constantly replayed.

The pictures that follow are from several collections.

Collection of 8 Hall of Fame busts from 1963 with 4 In their original boxes

Framed and autographed pictures and bats

Collection of game and game-used major league bats and batting gloves.

Game-worn major and minor league jerseys.

Dave Bergman Giants jersey and "Turn Back the Clock" jersey from 1991.

Will Clark's San Francisco jersey from his final season in 1993 and an autographed Ted Williams reproduction jersey.

Cincinnati Reds seat from Crosley Field and Federal league doll, c. 1914–15 from Buffalo, New York.

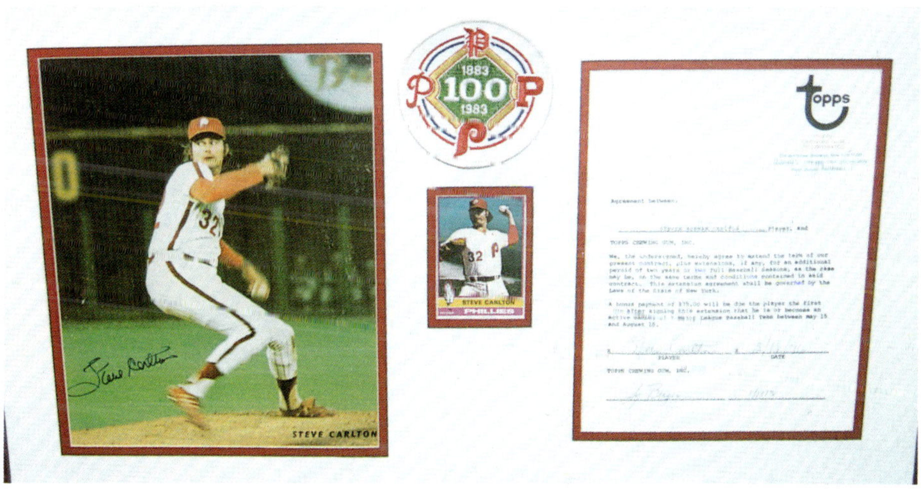

Signed contract between Steve Carlton and Topps for his 1976 baseball card.

Vintage St. Louis Browns pennant, c. 1950, and Red Sox pennant from 1948.

Collection of Ted Williams memorabilia.

Poster autographed by 13 members of the 3,000 Hit Club.

1987 baseball schedule with Ruth and autographs of 26 members of the Hall of Fame. When Mantle signed the piece, he commented "Now the Babe will be looking up at me."

Pictures from the George Kelly estate given to him by Gabby Hartnett and Joe McCarthy, framed with their black and white Hall of Fame plaques.

Autographed picture of Jimmy Foxx, a menu from his restaurant in Galesburg, Illinois, and a rare 1958 Foxx calendar from Brown and Bigelow.

Collection of Hartland statues, bats, and balls.

Pinch Hit Chewing Tobacco paper banner, c. 1930s, and set of five seats in original green paint from Crosley Field.

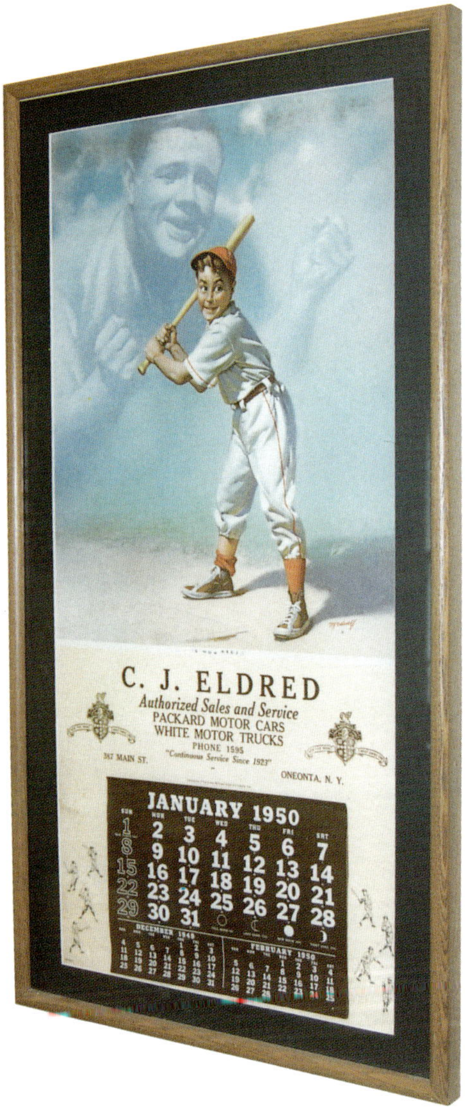

Initial calendar in the series of Babe Ruth from 1950. The calendars are difficult enough to find, but it becomes considerably more of a challenge if you are only interested in examples with all 12 months intact.

1952 Brown and Bigelow calendar of Connie Mack from the Hall of Fame series that went from 1950–1969.

Dizzy Dean "Spring Training" calendar art with government post card from Dean telling the sender that "I haven't pitched a no-hitter yet."

Honus Wagner poster "A Great Day" from Brown and Bigelow.

Cross-section of baseball memorabilia.

Baseball radio, Anniversary Hartland statue of Ruth, and rare Ruth Underwear box.

Collection of six individuals who spent a great deal of time tied to their seats during the making of *The Natural* in Buffalo, New York.

1960s National League Official Baseball Bag carried by the umpires for game balls.

Game and game-used baseball gloves.

Section of a room filled with baseball and other sports memorabilia.

Lou Gehrig "Dallas" Hartland box and Gehrig Hall of Fame plaque signed on the day his stamp was released in Cooperstown by Bart Giamatti and Mario Cuomo.

Ty Cobb photograph and check.

Collection of Hall of Fame induction bats.

Chapter 7

......Baseball Statues and Figurines

The Meandering Saga of Heartland Statues: A Collector's Perspective

By Lou Hagenbruch

Over the years many examples of Hartland misinformation have appeared in various publications, especially those which are sports-related, and recently over the Internet. What follows will be both a personal chronology of amassing a Hartland collection and an attempt to clear up the muddy waters of Hartland's history.

In the mid-1950s, the executives of Hartland Plastics, located just west of Milwaukee, decided to develop a line of baseball statues to provide additional work for the company during its down part of the year. At the time, the company was manufacturing items for breweries, auto parts, religious statuettes, and birthday cake figurines. Supervisor and designer Frank Fulop attended a great many major league baseball games at Milwaukee's County Stadium and Chicago's Comiskey Park in order to make numerous sketches of current stars of the game. From the sketches, the first prototypes were sculpted and molds manufactured in 1956–57. There were two copper molds for each player—one for the front and another for the back. In the spring of 1958 the first plastic baseball statues were released for sale. These were numbered as the company's 900 series.

That summer of 1958, I purchased my first Hartland baseball statue for $1.98 at a most unlikely place, the local shoe repairman's shop. Babe Ruth, the only non-current player at that time, was my first acquisition and the only statue in the display case. Bill, the owner/repairman, said one of the salesmen who provided him with supplies had left the Ruth statue to see if there was any interest. The next couple of times the salesman called on Bill, he left more statues. With money saved from baling hay and caddying, I was able to add players that I had seen play in person—Ted Williams, Stan Musial, Nellie Fox, and Luis Aparicio—and players I had seen play in the World Series on television—Mickey Mantle and Yogi Berra.

The more traditional locales with Hartlands for sale were major league baseball parks and department stores. Between my November birthday and Christmas that year my grandmother took me to Famous and Barr in downtown St. Louis. She bought Warren Spahn, Hank Aaron, Eddie Mathews, and Ernie Banks as presents for me.

During the spring of 1959, my dad and I painted a baseball field on a 3' by 4' piece of plywood with small wooden bases upon which to display my Hartland baseball players. I can still recall the day that I loaded the board and statues in the trunk of the car as my mother was getting ready to drive us across town to St. John's Grade School. I took it all to show to my eighth grade teacher, Sr. Michelle, and my fellow classmates. Early in the fall of '59, we moved to a larger house in another section of town. Not knowing that the boxes, small catalog/brochures, and tags would some day be worth a lot of money, I threw away all but one of each type of three brochures, and a corner of a box with the Hartland logo:

> A Hartland CREATION
> © Hartland PLASTICS, INC. 1958
> HARTLAND, WIS

Most of the boxes were the original style with a baseball scene, but some were of a more generic type—light in color with decorative markings—blue or black in color.

The board and statues were stored away and basically forgotten until Christmas season of 1963. While shopping in a local Gamble's department store, I saw three Hartlands for sale on a shelf in the basement section. I brought Don Drysdale, Rocky Colavito, and Dick Groat for $3.00 each. Following this purchase my interest and acquisition of Hartland baseball statues waned and in effect ceased until 1978–1979.

Hartland Plastics made four other baseball statues—Roger Maris, Harmon Killebrew, Willie Mays, and Duke Snider—in addition to the 14 baseball statues already mentioned. Within the set of 18 baseball statues a number of variations existed—three bat sizes, skin color, foot position, toe/foot plates or not, uniform numbers, and magnets on the feet. Also in their toy/statue line from the early 50s through the early 60s were numerous Western characters taken from movies and popular television programs of the time, along with a few historical figures, together considered the 800 series. The series featured two football stars in the early 60s—Johnny Unitas (Baltimore Colts) and Jon Arnett (Los Angeles Rams) and a generic lineman and running back in the colors of the NFL teams of that era. The reason for the generic football statues was simply the fact that Hartland only sold the Unitas and Arnett statues in the home city market of the respective player.

As far as the baseball statues are concerned, as few as 5,000 Groats and as many as 150,000 Aarons were manufactured and sold. Each statue is imprinted with "Hartland Plastics, Inc." in very small letters. Most imprints are on the back belt loop, but a few are in other locations such as the back of a sleeve. A metal Casey Stengel prototype had been completed and plans for a Jim Gentile statue were in the works when Hartland Plastics was bought out by the Revlon Cosmetic Company in 1964. The new owners had no interest in the statues and figurines. Consequently, most of the player molds and all related material were thrown into the trash, dumped, and buried in the city's dump. The company then made powder compacts and other cosmetic-related products until its closing in June of 1978. The Western molds were sold to the Strombecker company (later to be Steven Toys) in Hermann, Missouri. Unbeknownst until recent years, some of the original baseball player molds were in with the Western molds. For a short time the Strombecker company had the Western figures painted on an Indian reservation in Duran, Oklahoma. The quality of these figures was not very good, so production was stopped. These Western figures have since become known as "Durans".

As Hartland was shutting down, I again became interested in the baseball statues. The big baseball card and memorabilia craze of the mid-1980s was well underway, and I got somewhat caught up in the tide while trying to discover the monetary worth of my items that were boxed up and stored away. My first major interest was to complete my Hartland collection. Not knowing the company had closed, I dialed Directory Assistance for the Milwaukee area. There was a listing and I called the number. The lady that answered informed me of the company's closing, and gave me the number of someone who had worked for the company and might have some baseball statues for sale. On the subsequent call, I did reach a former female employee who had a Snider statue which I bought for $50. This was followed by the acquisition of Mays and an extra of both Spahn and Mantle from a friend at work for $25 to $35 apiece. Through an ad I placed in a local newspaper, I was able to purchase an extra Aparicio. Maris was had through a trade with a baseball card collector for a couple of 1957 and 1958 Topps cards and a set of the 1959 Ted Williams Fleer set (less card #68). The last of the statues, Killebrew, which I needed to complete my set of 18, came about through an ad in the *Sports Collectors Digest*. From a collector in Michigan, I acquired the Killebrew statue for $200—a little steep I thought, but it had been difficult finding anyone who would sell the statue, and I had a strong desire to have the set completed. It should be mentioned that Hartland Plastics did manufacture a smaller Little Leaguer (soon renamed "Bat Boy") that originally sold for 98 cents, and an even smaller minor leaguer appropriate for cake decoration. To me, these two items really were not a part of the player set, thus I had no desire to include them in my collection.

During the early 80s my interest again waned. I sold the extra Aparicio and Spahn to collectors, and traded the Mantle for numerous beer signs and tap handles.

Bill Alley, a Dallas lawyer with an interest in the Hartland statues, was able to acquire outstanding stock of the company during the mid to late 80s. With the technical assistance of Fulop—the aforementioned Hartland designer—Alley was able to get the company started again. The plan was to make a 25th Anniversary Commemorative set of the original 18 baseball statues. Original Hartlands from a private collection were brought in and computer-traced to create large (approximately 3" by 4") molds in steel. In a number of cases the cutting tools were not changed frequently enough, resulting in some of the features on the Commemoratives (especially facial) being blurred and rounded. The original statues looked almost exactly like the actual players, even down to the facial expressions. To distinguish the new statues from the originals, "25th" within a circle was imprinted on the back belt loop of each. Beginning in 1988, individual Commemorative figures or the entire set could be ordered by mail from Hartland Plastics, Inc., which had a Hartland, Wisconsin post office box, but Dallas address. If the entire set was ordered, then the "Bat Boy" was included free of charge. Things went well, and Nick Calcagno, an art professor at an Oklahoma university, was spotted by Fulop at a National Baseball Card Convention and employed by Alley to sculpt a new series of baseball player statues. Prototypes of Whitey Ford, Roberto Clemente, Dizzy Dean, Bob Feller, Lou Gehrig, Ty Cobb, Cy Young, Honus Wagner, Nolan Ryan, Carl Yastrzemski, and a confrontation between a manager and umpire were sculpted.

Initially all went well with the Commemoratives and the new line of statues. Alley employed Ron Glass in California to make the molds of Ford and Clemente. It is surmised the Alley was impatient and had the other molds, except for Yastrzemski, made somewhere in Dallas. As a result, the molds of Gehrig, Young, Wagner, and Ryan turned out quite different from those of Dean, Feller, Cobb, and the Confrontation. The statues of the former are taller, larger, and smoother in appearance, while the latter are shorter, slimmer, and somewhat chiseled in appearance. The molds for this new series were made from fiber-glass, and some of the statues were made hollow—Ford, Clemente, Young, and Wagner, while others were of solid plastic—Gehrig, Dean, Feller, Cobb, and the Confrontation. The company even started a newsletter in 1990 that was sent out approximately every two months to collectors who had ordered Commemoratives and/or new series statues. One of the newsletters gave collectors an opportunity to acquire Hartland-related items—pennants from the 1989 National Sports Collectors Convention in Chicago ($7.50), full color 10" by 14" Dealer Display Boards ($30), Commemorative boxes ($5.50) and unpainted assembled figures ($30)—to list a few. Plans for a book about Hartland's history was also in the planning stage. Hartland Plastics, Dallas, suddenly stopped in early 1991 when Alley, supposedly on a business trip to New York in February, disappeared. He could not be found, and left behind a pregnant wife and four children. Alley was located in Virginia during March 1992, but quickly vanished again.

Through a teaching colleague, Don Raycraft, I found out about the revival of Hartland Plastics in Dallas late in 1989. He and I quickly began purchasing the new series statues for $25 each, the same price as the commemorative. I had already received two Gehrigs (who I was named after), and one each of Ford, Clemente, and Dean by the time Alley pulled his disappearing act. Don, who had ordered his two Cobbs a month before me, was lucky enough to receive them just prior to the fiasco whereas I was not as fortunate. The packaging of these initial statues of the new series was superb—each statue in foam rubber wrapping within a zip-lock plastic bag enclosed in a thick, dark green box with a portrait of each particular player on the side.

Things at Hartland, Dallas, were in complete disarray—unpaid workers destroyed some of the molds and business halted for much of 1991. A letter dated August 5, 1991 was sent to Hartland collectors from Mrs. Pam Alley stating that effective July 3, 1991, many assets of Hartland Plastics, Inc., were sold to USA Hartland, Inc., owned by Bill Dunlap of Dallas. An undated letter including a brief history of Hartland followed and related to collectors that, with the supervision of Dunlap and his vice-president, Ken Movold, the aim of the new company was to get things back into production, finish the run of 10,000 each of the commemoratives, add new statues—including football player Johnny Unitas (to be made from original Hartland, Wisconsin molds), and start a collector's club. A large two page article about the new company and one page ad were printed in the February 14, 1992 issue of *Sports Collectors Digest*. In an attempt to retain collectors and their business, the new company offered to honor all pre-paid orders for new series statues with Commemoratives. To quickly meet the ensuing demand for Commemoratives, Dunlap had the molds shipped to China. The statues produced in China were painted with more pastel or lighter colors, and had "China" imprinted on a foot of each. Thus another variation was introduced into the Hartland saga. The China commemoratives are thought to be rarer than the Dallas Commemoratives.

In addition to Cobb, I had pre-paid orders sent in for Feller, Yaz, and the Confrontation. Through much of 1991 and early 1992, I exchanged a plethora of phone calls with various numbers and a multitude of letters with Hartland Plastics, Inc., and USA Hartland, Inc., in an attempt to find out what was transpiring and to get the statues I had ordered. I was even on a supposed waiting list for Cobb and Feller, but eventually had my name removed. Finally, I did receive five Commemoratives—Williams, Musial, Maris, Ruth, and Spahn, after sending in the shipping cost for each at $3.75. Each of the five Commemoratives had "China" imprinted on a shoe. I was able to acquire Cobb, Feller, and the Confrontation from Fulop who had completed a few of each from supplies sent to him at the closing of Hartland Plastics, Inc., and the beginning of USA Hartland, Inc. What few of these he had went quickly for $75 each. My collection of all original Hartlands, 1950s, 60s, as well as 1990s, was complete again. It had certainly been a hassle, but I was able to express a sigh of relief.

Things at USA Hartland, Inc., were moving again. Replacement Commemoratives for unfulfilled orders of Hartland Plastics, Inc., were shipped to customers. New one-page ads for baseball statues, most with 1992 copyright dates on them, were sent out to previous customers advertising commemoratives (color), Cy Young and Honus Wagner, Whitey Ford and Roberto Clemente, and Johnny Unitas and Anniversary Football players (all in black and white). A new, more professional looking newsletter was also sent out to advertise a number of items between August of 1991 to Fall of 1992. Then, in an undated letter (late 1992) Ken Movold announced as positive news that work was underway to restructure the company and upgrade its production capabilities. The letter went on to state that the company was "in the midst of consolidating the Hartland trademark (western and sports figurines) by moving...[its]...Dallas marketing office and fulfillment center to Hermann, Missouri so that all functions of the company...[could]...be under one roof and one management." This signaled the move of Hartland to Steven Toys.

While all of this was going on, I joined the Team Hartland Collector's Club with dues of $35. I can only recall paying the money once, but have a club ID card with a 4/95 expiration date. The card contains the serial number 050, which I assume probably meant that I was the fiftieth person to join. I received a free Hartland t-shirt and Hartland pennant as a club member for past inconveniences experienced. The Unitas statue that I received in December of 1992 was shipped from a Dallas Address, and the invoice stated that Wagner and Young would both be shipped on February 22, 1993. In any event, for $31.05 each ($34.50 to non-club members) I received the three statues as the transition to Hermann was underway. The boxes these figures came in were of thin cardboard, mainly gray in color, and each baseball player box included a red home plate design containing the player's name. Hartland and my collecting continued.

Hartland, a division of Steven Toys, had been located in a downtown factory building four blocks from the Missouri River. That all changed with the "Flood of '93" in July. The building was severely damaged to the point that the maintenance personnel and owners walked around on fallen walls to stay out of the flood water. Some things were salvaged, but almost everything was lost. A letter from Tim Ford, president and CEO, dated January 20, 1994 was sent out to collectors, and gave the impression that some new statues were being made. However, no Hartland baseball statues were manufactured after the flood. What had already been made and saved was simply painted, packaged and sent out to fill orders. While waiting for a permanent facility, bits and pieces of the business were scattered around town in a variety of buildings and warehouses. One building was across the river, and employees had to be transported to work by boat. The present (new) building was completed in the small industrial park on the hill above Hermann in 1995.

Prior to the flood in '93, Steven toys manufactured two types of Nolan Ryans, a Carl Yastrzemski, and three Yankee Commemorative statues (Berra, Mantle, and Maris). In addition to these, a small "Safe at Second"—two player, umpire and base set—was made of solid plastic figures. It had been decided to make Ryan in both home and away uniforms. The home style of Ryan in a solid box could be ordered through the company, whereas the away type in a display box had to be purchased in Target stores. The mold for the Yaz statue had not been made in Dallas and was not true to the original prototype. The original prototype was in the Red Sox home uniform and slim like Yaz himself. The final statue was in the Boston away uniform, and was robust to the point of looking similar to a pulling guard in football. The Yaz statue came in a display box similar to the Ryan display box. Ordered through the mail, Ryan and Yaz went for $37.50 each ($33.75 to club members) plus shipping ($3.50—1 statue, $5—2 statues, and $6.50—3 statues). The Ryan sold in Target stores went for $37.95. The three Commemoratives of the Yankees were sold in J.C. Penney stores along with Horse and Rider figures—Roy Rogers, Dale Evans, Wyatt Earp, George Washington, and Robert E. Lee. They all sold for $39.95, but did not sell well, so subsequently many were sold in outlet stores for $19.95. The latter statues, less the baseball Yankees, could also be purchased through the mail from Steven Toys. "Safe at Second" was manufactured from molds—made in Wisconsin in the early 60s—found in storage. This set sold through the mail for the same prices as Ryan and Yaz previously mentioned.

Before and after the flood, I managed to obtain the two Ryans, Yaz, and "Safe at Second", thereby assuring a complete set of first-run original Hartland baseball statues. The last of these came in a Commemorate Snider box with a "Safe at Second" label placed over Snider's name. Most had a professional multi-colored brochure/catalog enclosed that illustrated the baseball statues and Horse and Rider Series.

As stated before, no Hartland statues of any type have been manufactured since the flood. All statues and parts of statues have been sold, except for a few Earp figures on a horse. Between the flood and the present, the company has changed hands twice. The present owner who lives in Dallas took with him what few baseball statues there were in the company's collection. As of August 1998, the owner does not plan for Steven toys to produce any Hartlands. However, an employee who is primarily in sales, but also considers herself to be a part of miscellaneous and public relations, mentioned the fact that the owner is contemplating going onto the Internet to test the waters for interest in Hartland statues. The company has been averaging a total of 10 to 15 phone and mail inquiries a week concerning Hartlands. It has been rumored that Southland Plastics, Inc., a company that manufactures baseball statues, attempted to purchase the Hartland name, but the $1.5 million asking price was prohibitive. So it is anyone's guess what, if anything, will come to pass.

While visiting the Steven Toys plant in mid-June of '98, I purchased an Earp statue for $39.95—$41.73 with tax. Why, I am not really sure, other than the fact that it is the last Hartland of any type available for purchase from the company as opposed to buying from a collector or sports memorabilia shop.

Hartland Timeline

1953 Hartland Plastics Company of Hartland, Wisconsin begins to manufacture plastic statues of western television heroes. Included in the collection are Roy Rogers, the Lone Ranger, Tonto, and Dale Evans.

1957 Hartland executive Frank Fulop feels that a series of baseball statues would keep the production lines going during the winter and keep the workers employed.

1958 The baseball statues are offered for sale in the spring.

1959 Five thousand Johnny Unitas of the Baltimore Colts and Jon Arnett of the Los Angeles Rams statues are made. These are followed by a lineman and running back from each of the 14 NFL teams. These statues are not designed to be specific players.

Spring of 1960 Hartland statues are offered for sale for $2.98 each in the concession stands of major league parks. The players are paid $500 plus 5% of the gross sales. Some dime stores sell Hartlands for $1.98.

1963 Production of the baseball statues concludes when the company is sold to Revlon Cosmetics.

June 30, 1978 Revlon closes the plastics factory in Hartland, Wisconsin.

1987 William Alley of Dallas, Texas buys the rights to reproduce the original 18 Hartlands in a commemorative series of 10,000 of each player.

1990 The production of six additional statues, Clemente, Gehrig, Dean, Ford, Feller, Cobb, and "The Confrontation" is announced in Dallas. It is estimated the following numbers of statues were actually made:

Clemente and Ford—10,000
Gehrig and Dean*—500
Cobb*—45
Feller—25
"The Confrontation"—20

*We received Gehrig, Dean, and Cobb in the mail with our subscription, so the estimated numbers may be conservative.

March 1991 Alley goes to New York City and disappears. The company shuts down and on July 3, 1991 Alley's wife sells the company to Bill Dunlap who renames it USA Hartland Inc. USA Hartland Inc. is sold to Steven Manufacturing of Hermann, Missouri. Steven releases Ryan, Young, Wagner, Yastrzemski, and "Safe at Second".

July 8, 1993 Steven Manufacturing is destroyed in a massive flood.

October 18, 1993 A letter is sent to subscribers explaining the problem with the flood and indicating that Steven will be back in business shortly. At this writing Steven is *not* producing Hartland statues.

Hartland Q & A with RC Raycraft

What is the single rarest Hartland?

A single metal prototype of Casey Stengel was made but never manufactured. Jim Gentile was also in the initial stage of design when the company was sold to Revlon.

How rare are the Feller and "The Confrontation"?

Probably less than 25 of each exist.

Are there many variations with the statues?

Among many are several listed below:

Nolan Ryan is found a home and road uniform. The gray (road) Ryan was produced to sell at Target stores. There were approximately 5500 road Ryans and 4500 home versions.

Eleven of the statues were made with magnets on the foot or metal base. These were designed to be used on the dashboard of your father's 1960 Buick. The 11 include Aaron, Banks, Berra, Fox, Mantle, Mathews, Mays, Musial, Ruth, Spahn, and the minor leaguer.

Williams can be found with "Red" or "Reds" on his jersey.

Fox and Aparicio may or may not have red trim around the "Sox" on their jersey front or around the number of the back. They also were made with and without toe plates.

There are three distinct sizes of bats that were produced:

Regular Bat
Aaron
Colavito
Killebrew
Mantle
Snider
Williams

Shorter Bat
Banks
Groat
Musial
Maris

"Bulbous" Long Bat
Ruth

Why do some of the original Hartlands appear to be yellow or jaundiced rather than white?

The statues made with recycled plastic by Hartland in Wisconsin tend to yellow over time.

Which of the original 18 are the most commonly found?

The Aaron, Mathews, and Spahn since they played in Milwaukee and the statues were manufactured in Hartland, Wisconsin.

Which of the original statues are the most difficult to find?

The only two who are not in the Hall of Fame—Groat and Colavito. There were approximately 5,000 Groat statues manufactured and approximately 10,000 Colavito statues.

Did Hartland "stamp" the statues?

On the majority of the statues the stamp was placed on the back belt loop of the player's pants, but there were some variations in the stamping also. Williams' stamp is behind his shoulder, Colavito's is under his shoulder, Mantle's stamp is on the inside of his right arm. On the reproduction Hartlands the stamp is on the back of the player's belt.

What was the original selling price of the commemorative statues?

$25-30

Which of the numbered statues are called the "Dallas" Hartlands?

Clemente, Cobb, "The Confrontation", Dean, Feller, and Ford.

Which are considered to be the "Missouri" Hartlands?

Ryan (home and away), "Safe at Second", Wagner, Young, and Yastrzemski; Clemente and Ford statues were also made in Hermann, Missouri.

Which of the Hartlands from the 1950s are generating the most interest among collectors?

Dick Groat, Duke Snider, Don Drysdale, Rocky Colavito, and Harmon Killebrew are probably the most collectible today. The Snider and Drysdale were sold primarily in the Los Angeles area like Mathews, Spahn, and Aaron were sold in the Midwest, especially in Wisconsin. There were less than 5,000 Groats made and he was not a huge fan favorite at the time.

Values of Dallas Hartland Statues

Player	Value
Bob Feller	$2,000–3,000 (add $400–500 with box)
Dizzy Dean	$200–300 (with box)
Lou Gehrig	$225–325 (with box)
Roberto Clemente	$125–175 (with green box)
Ty Cobb	$900–1,200 (add $500–600 with box)
Whitey Ford	$100-120 (with box)
"The Confrontation"	$2,000 (add $1,000 with box)

Values of Missouri Hartland Statues

Player	Value
Carl Yastrzemski	$400–575 (with box)
Nolan Ryan (home or away)	$75–100 (with box)
Roberto Clemente	$125–150 (with gray box)
Honus Wagner	$150–175
Cy Young	$150–175
"Safe at Second"	$115–125

Evaluating Original Hartland Statues

To establish a price for a Hartland statue it is critical to include the following in the evaluation process:

- Are all of the original pieces (bats, toe plates, catcher's mask, etc.) with the statue?
- Are the original colors still vibrant?
- Has the statue faded or the plastic turned yellow over time?
- Has there been any kind of repair or repainting to the statue?
- What is the degree of rarity of the statue?
- Does the statue still have its original tag or box?

The eighteen original Hartland baseball statues, the bat boy, and the minor leaguer that are priced below should be considered to be in "very good" to "excellent" condition. All the statues are intact and have strong color. The plastic statues have not faded or yellowed. They do not have their original boxes or tags.

Player	Value	Approximate No. Issued
Henry Aaron	$225–300	150,000
Louis Aparicio	$250–300	100,000
Ernie Banks	$250–300	75,000
Yogi Berra	$275–300	150,000
Rocky Colavito	$850–1000	10,000
Don Drysdale	$400–485	75,000
Nelson Fox	$225–275	100,000
Dick Groat	$1400–1600	5,000
Harmon Killebrew	$400–485	35,000
Mickey Mantle	$350–400	150,000
Roger Maris	$400–475	100,000
Eddie Mathews	$225–285	150,000
Willie Mays	$275–325	150,000
Stan Musial	$250–300	100,000
Babe Ruth	$225–275	150,000
Duke Snider	$400–475	75,000
Warren Spahn	$225–275	150,000
Ted Williams	$300–375	150,000
Bat Boy	$175–200	20,000
Minor Leaguer	$125–150	20,000

Values of the 25th Anniversary Set of Hartland Statues

The statues below are assumed to be in at least "excellent" to "near mint" condition and have their original boxes. The advertised number of each of the original 18 players in the Anniversary Set of Hartland statues was 10,000.

Player	Value
Aaron	$95–120
Aparicio	$70–85
Banks	$60–75
Berra	$90–110
Colavito	$60–75
Drysdale	$75–85
Fox	$50–65
Groat	$60–75
Killebrew	$85–100
Mantle	$100–125
Maris	$100–125
Mathews	$75–90
Musial	$80–90
Mays	$100–120
Ruth	$70–85
Snider	$70–85
Spahn	$60–80
Williams	$100–120
Bat Boy	$120–140
Minor Leaguer	$140–165

Hall of Fame Plastic Busts

The Sports Hall of Fame Inc. of Lynbook, L.I., New York manufactured twenty plastic busts of baseball greats in 1963. They were sold in toy stores, candy shops, and baseball parks. The busts were met with mixed success and were being offered at the sale price of 10 for $10 in the March 1965 issue of *Baseball Magazine*.

The busts were produced in two series with ten players in each. The lack of success of the initial series apparently limited the interest in the second series because they are difficult to find today.

Busts in Series I are typically found in the $65–100 price range with an additional $25 added to the price if the original box is included. The Series II busts should be available at some point between $125–200. The most common of the Series II busts are Jackie Robinson and Bob Feller. Hank Greenberg and Jimmy Foxx are the toughest to locate. Foxx is especially rare and is probably going to be valued at $225–300. If the Series II bust comes with an original box, add $50–75 to the price.

Series I 1963 HOF Busts	Series II 1963 HOF Busts
Christy Mathewson	Hank Greenberg
Walter Johnson	Jimmy Foxx
Pie Traynor	Paul Waner
Bill Dickey	John McGraw
Honus Wagner	Joe Cronin
Rogers Hornsby	Bob Feller
Lou Gehrig	Tris Speaker
Ty Cobb	Mickey Cochrane
Joe DiMaggio	George Sisler
Babe Ruth	Jackie Robinson

Dean Anniversary Hartland box

Metz Statues

Metz statues were manufactured in Rockford, Illinois and offered for sale in early 1987. Metz was attempting to fill a void in the marketplace left by Hartland, who went out of the baseball statue business in 1963. They didn't.

Metz apparently had signed contracts with Vince Coleman, Eddie Mathews, Jose Canseco, Ozzie Smith, Wade Boggs, Jack Clark, Whitey Ford, and Eric Davis. They also produced a statue of Eureka College's most famous athlete, Ronald Reagan.

Anniversary Dizzy Dean Hartland statue. $275

Roberto Clemente Anniversary Hartland—$135

Roger Maris Hartland statue, c. 1960. $475

Clemente Anniversary box.

Stan Musial Anniversary Hartland. $85

Mickey Mantle Anniversary statue. $100

Ted Williams Anniversary statue. $110

Rare Ted Williams Anniversary statue that was never painted. These were offered for sale by Dallas Hartland when it was facing serious financial difficulties. $150–175

1960 Hartland statues of Yogi Berra ($300) and Ted Williams ($350).

1960 Willie Mays Hartland. $300

1960 Yogi Berra Hartland. $300

1960 Don Drysdale Hartland. $450

Luis Aparicio, c. 1960
Hartland. $250

Nellie Fox, c. 1960 Hartland. $250

Henry Aaron, c. 1958 Hartland. $235

Eddie Mathews, Hartland statue c. 1958. $225

The manager in "The Confrontation" was supposedly modeled after Sparky Anderson.

"Dallas" Confrontation Anniversary statue. This exceedingly rare Hartland is one of less than 25 that were made in Dallas and is valued at approximately $2000.

Rare Bob Feller Anniversary Hartland. $2500

It is estimated that there are no more than 25 Feller Hartland statues.

Ernie Banks, c. 1960 Hartland statue. $275

Signatures of Hartland designer Frank Fulop and Bob Feller on the base of the Feller "Dallas" Hartland.

Close-up of Banks Hartland

"Dallas" Hartland statue of a sliding Ty Cobb, $1000. It is estimated that only 45 of the 10,000 statues scheduled for production were ever released.

Babe Ruth, c. 1960. $250

Rare "Dallas" Hartland box of Cobb. The Cobb boxes are valued at about $500.

Anniversary Babe Ruth statue. $75. Take a moment and compare that two statues that were made 30 years apart. The original Hartland is much more detailed in the face when compared with the "softer" features of the Anniversary example.

Lou Gehrig "Dallas" Hartland. $225–250

Anniversary minor leaguer.
$125–150

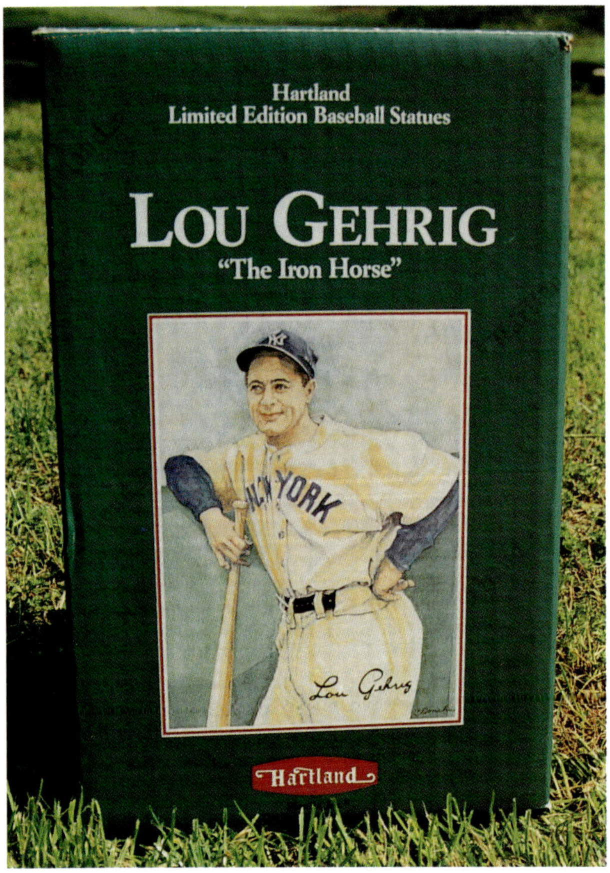

Lou Gehrig "Dallas" green box

Anniversary bat boy Hartland given to subscribers. $175

The rarest of the original c. 1960 Hartlands was Pirate shortstop Dick Groat. $1400–1600

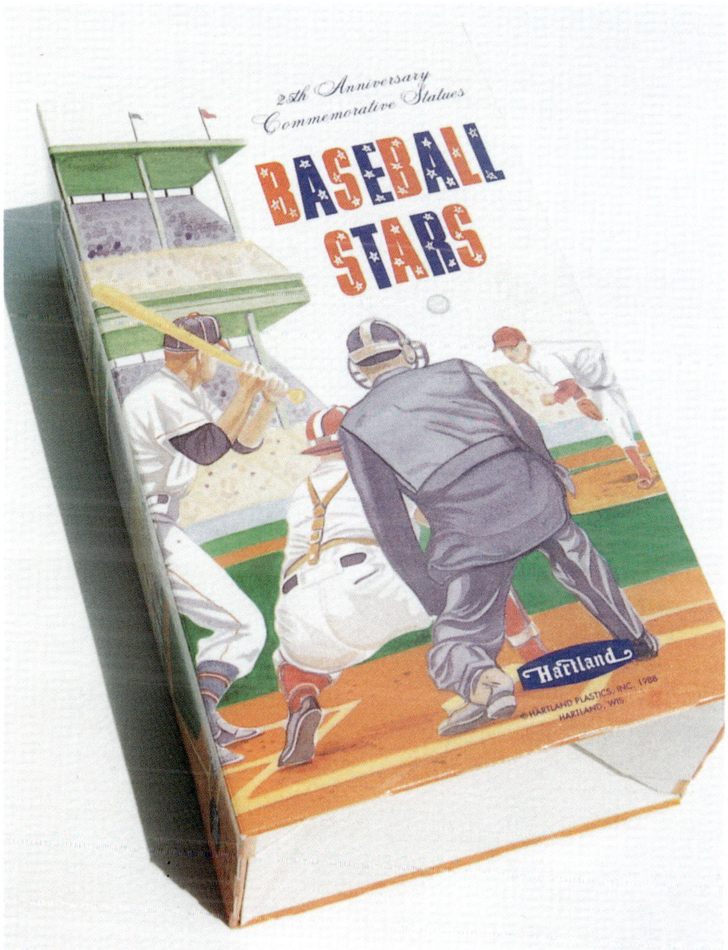

Anniversary Hartland box of Dick Groat

Top of Anniversary Dick Groat box with printed autograph.

Original Hartland statue of the winningest left-handed pitcher of all-time, Warren Spahn. $250

John McGraw and Ty Cobb called Honus Wagner the greatest shortstop of all-time. The Wagner Hartland was made in Hermann, Missouri shortly before the factory closed. $150

This Cy Young statue was also produced in Hermann, Missouri. Young won 511 games during his long career. $175

"Dallas" Whitey Ford statue. $115

Original Duke Snider statue. $400–475

Original Rocky Colavito statue.
$850–1000

"Missouri" Safe at Second. $115

Safe at Second label over a Duke Snider Anniversary box.

Babe Ruth appears to be directing the other seventeen original Hartland statues c. 1960 from a backyard in Clinton, Illinois. $8000–11,000 (set of 18).

T-shirt given to members of the Hartland Collectors Club c. 1992.

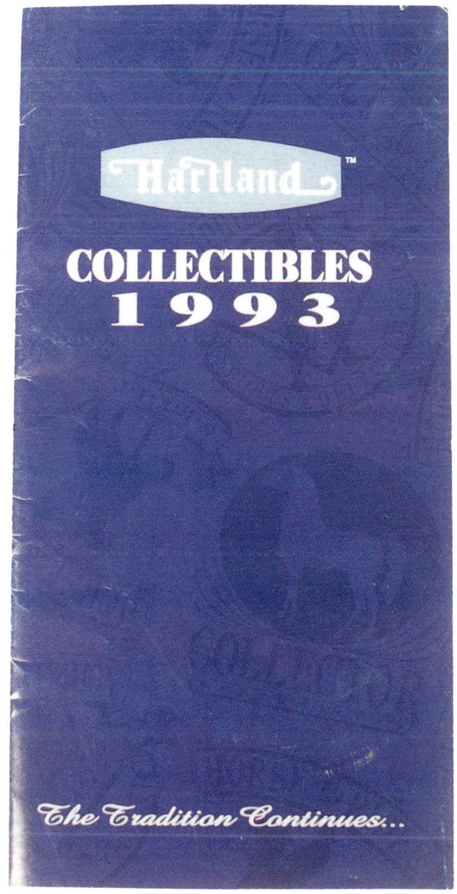

Hartland Collectibles catalog from 1993.

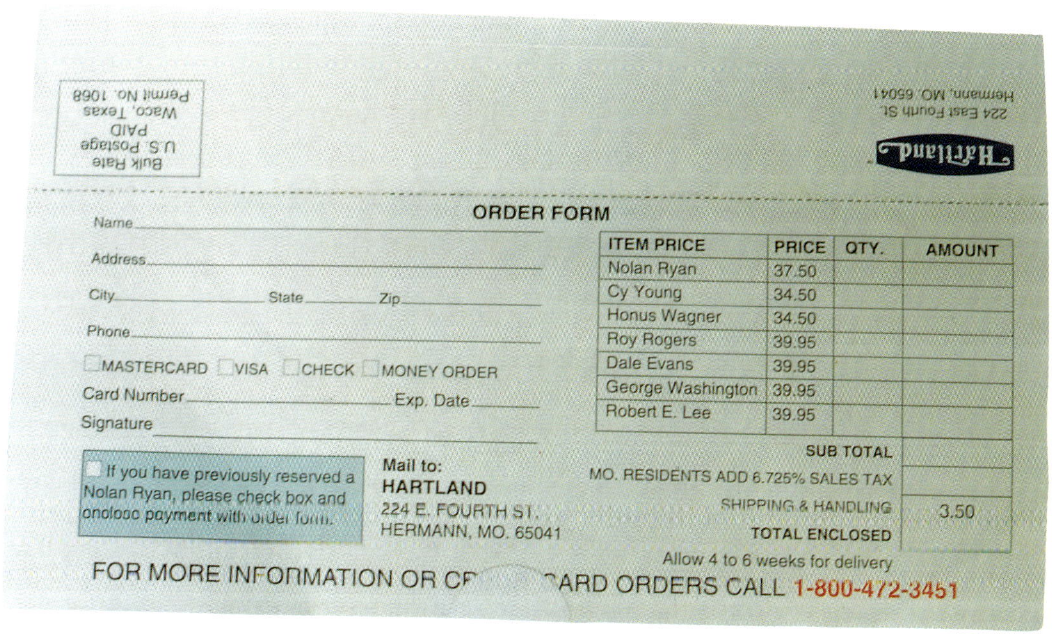

Bulk Rate
U.S. Postage
PAID
Waco, Texas
Permit No. 1068

Hartland
224 East Fourth St.
Hermann, MO. 65041

ORDER FORM

Name__________
Address__________
City_____ State_____ Zip_____
Phone__________
☐MASTERCARD ☐VISA ☐CHECK ☐MONEY ORDER
Card Number__________ Exp. Date_____
Signature__________

ITEM PRICE	PRICE	QTY.	AMOUNT
Nolan Ryan	37.50		
Cy Young	34.50		
Honus Wagner	34.50		
Roy Rogers	39.95		
Dale Evans	39.95		
George Washington	39.95		
Robert E. Lee	39.95		
		SUB TOTAL	
		MO. RESIDENTS ADD 6.725% SALES TAX	
		SHIPPING & HANDLING	3.50
		TOTAL ENCLOSED	

☐ If you have previously reserved a Nolan Ryan, please check box and enclose payment with order form.

Mail to:
HARTLAND
224 E. FOURTH ST.
HERMANN, MO. 65041

Allow 4 to 6 weeks for delivery

FOR MORE INFORMATION OR C[illegible]ARD ORDERS CALL 1-800-472-3451

Order blank for the "Missouri" Hartlands.

Felt Hartland pennant from the early 1990's.

Anniversary Hartland advertising brochure that indicates that Drysdale, Williams, and Musial were the first to sell out in an edition of 10,000 statues.

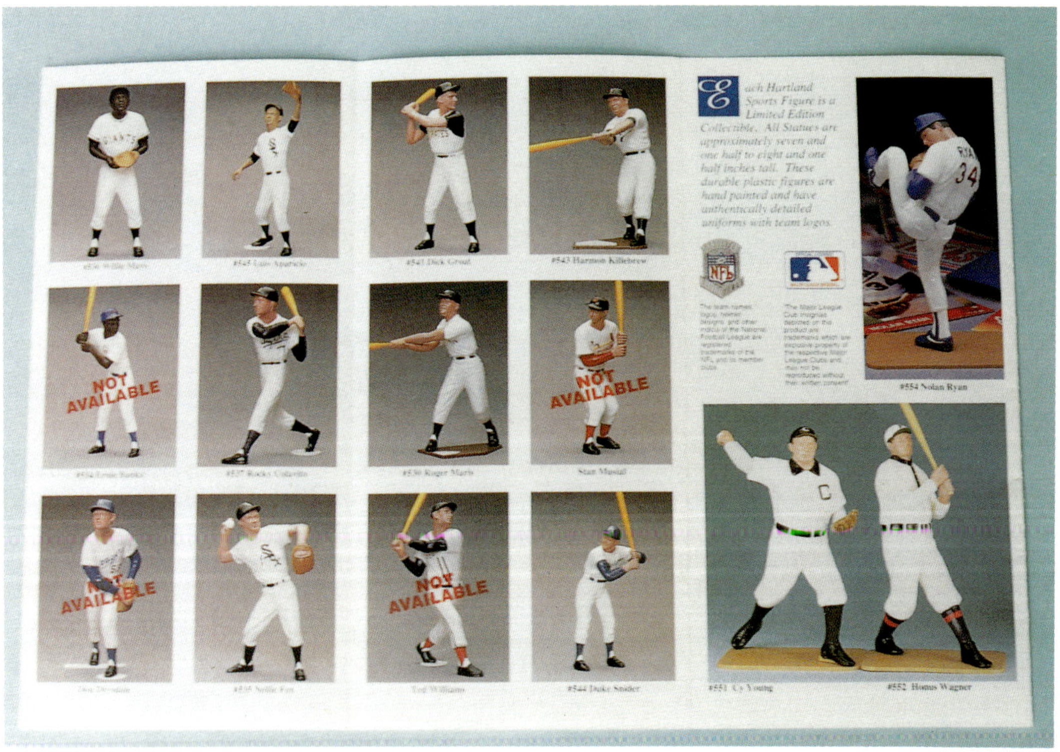

Advertisement for the "Missouri" Hartlands listing only 12 of the anniversary Hartlands and Ryan, Wagner, and Young. Of the twelve anniversary Hartlands, Banks, Musial, Drysdale, and Williams were already sold out.

Honus Wagner

Reverse side of the Wagner bust.

Bill Dickey

Walter Johnson

Joe DiMaggio

Jackie Robinson

Reverse side of the DiMaggio bust.

Rare Hank Greenberg bust.

Bob Feller bust.

Tris Speaker bust.

Babe Ruth bust.

Ty Cobb bust from Series I.

Original box with Rogers Hornsby bust.

Original box with Christy Mathewson bust.

Reverse side of the box (from previous page) showing players from Series I and II.

Metz statue of Jose Canseco

The muscular back of Canseco.

Vince Coleman edges off base.

Whitey Ford in the original Metz box.

Reverse of the Ford box listing his statistics.

Chapter 8

Sources

Networking is absolutely essential for success as a collector of baseball memorabilia. Let people know your interests. Uncle Ned may have brought home a program from the 1944 World Series in St. Louis or a press pin from Cleveland in 1954. If you are short on relatives, consult the list that follows:

Auctions

Leland's
36 East 22nd St. 7th Floor
New York, NY 10010
Comment: Offers a heavily illustrated color catalog of its baseball and major sports-related auctions.

Baseball Autographs

Richard Albersheim
1498-M Reistertown Rd. #201
Baltimore, MD 21208
410-358-9130

Ron Gordon
4900 Modoc Rd.
Las Cruces, NM 88011

Mark Jordan
1000 Ballpark Way #306
Arlington, TX 76011

Kevin Keating
P.O. Box 25274
Alexandria, VA 22314

James Spence III
130 Brookshire Lane
Orwigsburg, PA 17961

Greg Tucker
P.O. Box 909
Broken Arrow, OK 74013-0909

Baseball Autographs of Specific Players

Several Hall of Fame players have developed businesses that offer their signatures on a variety of items. They also have established autograph rates on specific items that can be mailed to them.

Yogi Berra
LTD
375 Rt. 10E
Whipparry, NY 07981

Reggie Jackson
Mr. October Foundation
305 Amador Ave.
Seaside, CA 93955
Comment: The Mr. October Foundation was established as a charitable organization to provide academic assistance to elementary and high school students.

Stan Musial
Stan the Man Inc.
1650 Des Peres Rd.
Suite 125
St. Louis, MO 63131

Baseball Cards

Larry Fritsch Cards
735 Old Wausau Rd.
PO Box 863 Dept. 287
Stevens Point, WI 54481
Comment: 200 page catalog available

Bill Henderson Cards
2320 Ruger Ave.
Janesville, WI 53545
Comment: Cards from 1948–89

Kit Young Cards
11535 Sorrento Valley Rd. #403
San Diego, CA 92121
Comment: Catalog and cards from 1949-1973

Baseball Games (Collectible and Antique)

Mark Cooper
816 Chauncey Road
Penn Valley, PA 19072

Baseball-Related Music

Holley Music
52 Pioneer St.
Cooperstown, NY 13320
Comment: A catalog is available of rare and unusual compact discs, cassettes, and CD-ROMS that contain baseball music and actual game recordings.

Baseball Tours

Jay Buckley
Box 213
LaCrosse, WI 54602
Comment: A respected travel agency that offers a wide variety of innovative air and bus tours to major league baseball games with accommodations, side trips, and game tickets.

Baseball Videos

Rare Sportsfilms
1126 Tennyson Lane
Naperville, IL 60540

Comment: A catalog of baseball-related videos that includes World Series, All-Star, and team issues high light films from the 1930s to today.

Bobbing Head Dolls

Tim Hunter
4301 W. Hidden Valley Dr.
Reno, NV 89502

Game-Used Equipment and Uniforms

Murf Denny
Box 127
Brule, WI 54820
(catalog)

Robb Wochnick
PO Box 388
Wilsonville, OR 97070
(catalog)

Wayne Otto
PO Drawer 2628
Boone, NC 28607

Kim Stigall
Ball Park Heroes
1531 J. Street
Bedford, IN 47421

MeiGray Group
744 Mountain Blvd.
Watchung, NJ 07060

National Baseball Hall of Fame

The Librarian
National Baseball Hall of Fame
P.O. Box 590
Cooperstown, NY 13326
Comment: More than 400,000 baseball photos on file that may be purchased

Gift Shop Mail Order
National Baseball Hall of Fame
P.O. Box 540
Cooperstown, NY 13326-0590
888-425-5633 (toll free)

Publications

Society for American Baseball Research (SABR)
P.O. Box 93183
Cleveland, OH 44101-5183

Vintage and Classic Baseball Collector Magazine
P.O. Box 39366
Tacoma, WA 98439-0366

Robert Crestohl
4732 Circle Rd.
Montreal, Quebec, Canada H3W-121
Comment: Complete yearly runs of the Sporting News, baseball guides, and magazines

Jeff Whitmore
P.O. Box 7061
Richmond, VA 23221
Comment: An exceptional newsletter that provides information about autograph signings, show insights, and "inside" hobby information.

Sports Collectors Digest
700 E. State
Iola, WI 54990
Comment: Published weekly with each issue approaching or exceeding 200 pages.

Ticket Stubs and Programs

Bob Adelson
13610 N. Scottsdale Rd. #10
Scottsdale, AZ 85254

Major League Baseball Addresses

Major League Baseball
350 Park Ave.
New York, NY 10022
(212) 339-7800

American League
350 Park Ave.
New York, NY 10022
(212) 339-7600

Baltimore Orioles
333 W. Camden St.
Baltimore, MD 21201

Boston Red Sox
Fenway Park
24 Yawkey Way
Boston, MA 02215

California Angels
P.O. Box 2000
Anaheim, CA 92803

Chicago White Sox
333 W. 35th Street
Chicago, IL 60616

Cleveland Indians
2401 Ontario St.
Cleveland, OH 44114-40003

Detroit Tigers
2121 Trumbull Ave.
Detroit, MI 48216

Kansas City Royals
P.O. Box 419969
Kansas City, MO 64141

Minnesota Twins
34 Kirby Puckett Place
Minneapolis, MN 55415

New York Yankees
Yankee Stadium
Bronx, NY 10451

Oakland Athletics
Oakland Coliseum
Oakland, CA 94621

Seattle Mariners
P.O. Box 4100
Seattle, WA 98104

Tampa Bay Devil Rays
One Tropicana Dr.
St. Petersburg, FL 33705

Texas Rangers
P.O. Box 1111
Arlington, TX 76010

Toronto Blue Jays
The Sky Dome
300 Bremner Blvd. Suite 3200
Toronto Ontario, Canada M5V-3B3

National League
350 Park Ave.
New York, NY 10022
(212) 339-7700

Arizona Diamondbacks
400 N. Fifth St. Suite 1100
Phoenix, AZ 85004

Atlanta Braves
P.O. Box 4064
Atlanta, GA 30302

Chicago Cubs
1060 W. Addison St.
Chicago, IL 60613

Cincinnati Reds
100 Riverfront Stadium
Cincinnati, OH 45202

Colorado Rockies
1700 Broadway, Suite 2100
Denver, CO 80290

Florida Marlins
2267 NM 199th St.
Miami, FL 33056-2600

Houston Astros
P.O. Box 288
Houston, TX 77001-0288

Los Angeles Dodgers
1000 Elysian Park Ave.
Los Angeles, CA 90012

Milwaukee Brewers
Milwaukee County Stadium
Milwaukee, WI 53214

Montreal Expos
P.O. Box 500 Station M
Montreal, Quebec, Canada HIV-3P2

New York Mets
Shea Stadium
Flushing, NY 11368

Philadelphia Phillies
P.O. Box 7575
Philadelphia, PA 19101

Pittsburgh Pirates
Three Rivers Stadium
Pittsburgh, PA 15212

St. Louis Cardinals
250 Stadium Plaza
St. Louis, MO 63102

San Diego Padres
P.O. Box 2000
San Diego, CA 92120

San Francisco Giants
Candlestick Park
San Francisco, CA 94124

Web Sites

Major League Baseball
http://www.majorleaguebaseball.com
Hall of Fame
http://www.baseballhalloffame.org

Sites for Sports Webcasts and Audio Feeds

http://www.audionet.com
http://www.cbssportsline.com
http://www.cnnsi.com
http://www.finalfour.net
http://www.sportsticker.com
http://espn.sportzone.com
http://www.totalsports.com

Spring Training Addresses

Arizona
Arizona Diamondbacks
Tucson Electric Park
2500 E. Ajo Way
Tucson, AZ 85713

Anaheim Angels
2200 W. Alameda
Tempe, AZ 85282

Oakland Athletics
Phoenix Municipal Stadium
5999 E. Van Buren
Phoenix, AZ 85008

Chicago Cubs
HoHoKam Park
1235 N. Center St.
Mesa, AZ 85201

Chicago White Sox
Tucson Electric Park
Kino Veterans Sports Park
2500 E. Ajo Way
Tucson, AZ 85713

San Diego Padres
16101 N. 83rd Ave.
Peoria, AZ 85382

Milwaukee Brewers
Maryville Baseball Park
3600 N. 51st Ave.
Phoenix, AZ 85061

Seattle Mariners
Peoria Stadium
16101 N. 83rd Ave.
Peoria, AZ 85382

Colorado Rockies
Hi Corbett Field
3400 E. Camino Campestre
Tucson, AZ 85716

San Francisco Giants
Scottsdale Stadium
7408 E. Osborn Road
Scottsdale, AZ 85251

Florida
Toronto Blue Jays
Dunedin Stadium at Grant Field
311 Douglas Ave.
Dunedin, FL 34698

Cincinnati Reds
Ed Smith Stadium
2700 12th St.
Sarasota, FL 34237

Houston Astros
Osceola County Stadium
1000 Bill Beck Blvd.
Kissimmee, FL 34744

Montreal Expos
Roger Dean Stadium
4751 Main St.
Jupiter, FL 33458

Philadelphia Phillies
Jack Russell Stadium
800 Phillies Drive
Clearwater, FL 34615

St. Louis Cardinals
Roger Dean Stadium
4751 Main St.
Jupiter, FL 33458

Baltimore Orioles
Ft. Lauderdale Stadium
5301 NW 12th Ave.
Ft. Lauderdale, FL 33309

Detroit Tigers
Joker Marchant Stadium
2301 Lakeland Hills Blvd.
Lakeland, FL 33805

Minnesota Twins
Lee County Sports Complex
14100 Six Mile Cypress Pkwy.
Fort Myers, FL 33912

Texas Rangers
Charlotte County Stadium
2300 El Jobean Road
Port Charlotte, FL 33948

Atlanta Braves
710 S. Victory Way
Kissimmee, FL 34747

Florida Marlins
5600 Stadium Parkway
Melbourne, FL 32940

Los Angeles Dodgers
Holman Stadium
4101 26th St.
Vero Beach, FL 32960

New York Mets
525 NW Peacock Blvd.
Port St. Lucie, FL 34986

Pittsburgh Pirates
McKechnie Field
1611 9th St. West
Bradenton, FL 34208

New York Yankees
Legends Field
1 Steinbrenner Dr.
Tampa, FL 33614

Boston Red Sox
City of Palms Park
2201 Edison Ave.
Fort Myers, FL 33901

Cleveland Indians
Chain O'Lakes Park
Cypress Gardens Blvd.
Winter Haven, FL 33880

Kansas City Royals
Baseball City Stadium
300 Stadium Way
Davenport, FL 33837

Tampa Bay Devil Rays
Al Lang Stadium
180 2nd Ave. SE
St. Petersburg, FL 33701

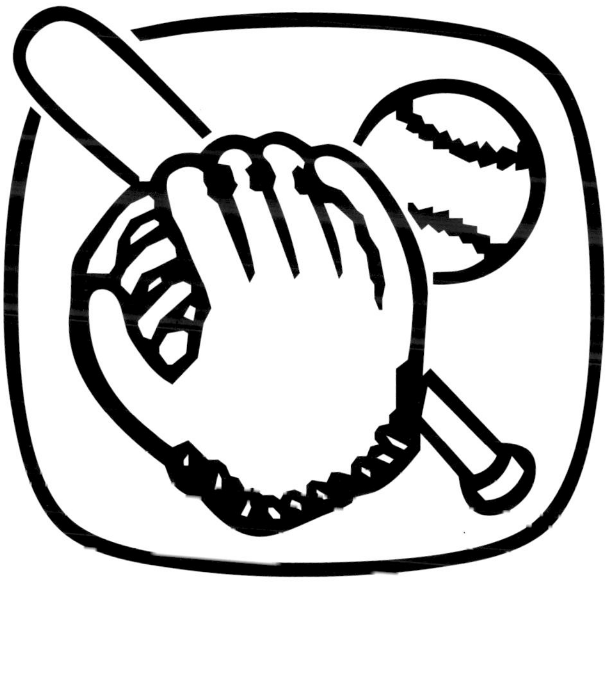

10 Best and Worst Baseball Movies of All-Time

Nationally known television and film critic Jeffery Ellish of Champaign, Illinois has picked the best and worst baseball films (in no particular order) exclusively for this book.

Best

Bingo Long Traveling All-Stars and Motor Kings (1976)
Bull Durham (1988)
Cobb (1994)
Eight Men Out (1988)
Field of Dreams (1989)
League of Their Own (1992)
Long Gone (1987, made for television)
The Natural (1984)
The Pride of the Yankees (1942)
Tiger Town (1983, made for television)

Worst

Angels in the Outfield (1951 & 1994)
The Babe (1992)
The Babe Ruth Story (1948)
Comrades of Summer (1992)
The Fan (1996)
Fear Strikes Out (1957)
Kid from Left Field (1979)
Major League II (1994)
Major League III (1998)
Mr. Destiny (1990)

All-Time Worst Casting in a Baseball Film

John Goodman as the teenage Babe Ruth
William Bendix as Babe Ruth
Michael Caine in Mr. Destiny
Tony Perkins as Jimmy Piersall

Chapter 9

Glossary of Collecting Related Terms

3 x 5 (lined or unlined)—A 3-inch by 5-inch card that may have a lined side and a blank side. Autograph collectors prefer that the signature be on the unlined side of the card.

ALS—A letter that has been signed.

Autopen—A mechanical device that is programmed to duplicate a precise signature. Autopens are often used by show business, sports, and political celebrities who receive numerous requests for their autographs.

cachet—A specially designed and produced envelope to commemorate a specific historical or sporting event that is usually postmarked on the anniversary or actual day of the event.

certificate of authenticity—A piece of paper, usually of minimal value, that guarantees that the signature or piece of memorabilia that you purchased is authentic or legitimate.

cut—A signature that has been literally "cut" away from the check, card, or letter on which it was originally written.

F.D.C.—An envelope or cachet that is designed to be postmarked to celebrate a specific event on the day or anniversary of the event. F.D.C. stands for "first day cover".

find—A "find" usually occurs several times in a collector's career. It is similar to having a blind date and the homecoming queen answers the door. A "find" normally happens because of a chance encounter or casual comment that results in your being able to purchase something for your collection of exceptional quality for a favorable and economical price. What makes the "find' possible is that simple fact that people look upon baseball in a special way and tend to keep scorecards, autographs, and other odd pieces of memorabilia they accumulate over the years that eventually turn into a treasure for someone else. The belief that most "finds" have already been found is not true. They are still out there waiting for all of us who continue the hunt.

flat—A term used at autograph shows to describe a picture, poster, magazine, postcard, or card. Usually "flats" have a different pricing structure than equipment, uniforms, or balls.

game—A uniform, hat, or piece of equipment manufactured and designed for use in a college or professional game or sporting event. A "game" bat was ordered by the player to be used but is not "game used" until it actually makes its way into the batter's box.

game-used or game-worn—A uniform, hat, or piece of equipment actually used or worn in a college or professional sporting event.

GPC—The initials GPC stand for "government postcard". These pre-stamped postcards were especially popular for obtaining autographs by mail from the 1930s through the 1950s. A fan waiting outside the stadium could hand the self-addressed postcard to the player for his signature at a more convenient time.

Hall of Fame plaque—A postcard that is a duplicate of the individual plaque that honors a member of the Baseball Hall of Fame in Cooperstown, N.Y. The HOF plaques of every member are sold in the gift shop of the Hall of Fame.

matted out—A term used in the framing process to describe the covering of something not wanted in the finished product. For example, if a 3 x 5 card is personalized to "Robert" and your name is "Bill", you would probably want Robert's name matted out.

minimum bid—The lowest acceptable offer that an auctioneer will take for a particular item to begin the auction.

National—A sports memorabilia show held each year in a different section of the United States that draws thousands of people and more than 700 dealers.

paint pen—Gold or silver markers with opaque ink that can be difficult to use because of inconsistent ink flow, potential for getting on clothing, and general unreliability.

private signing—An autographing event where an individual employs a celebrity to sign a number of items or "pieces" that have been mailed in or ordered by collectors. A private signing is not a public event.

provenance—The history of ownership of a particular item. Allows the buyer to secure additional insight as to the origins of the piece.

SASE—self-addressed stamped envelope

SCD—*Sports Collectors Digest* is published weekly from Iola, Wisconsin.

Sharpie—A permanent marker made by Sanford in a variety of colors and pen points for use with cloth, paper, or leather.

Single-signed—An item (often a ball) with only one autograph.

stamped—An autograph applied to a photograph, card, or ball with a rubber stamp, not hand signed.

sweet spot/manager's spot—The section of a baseball reserved for the manager on team-signed balls. It is also the most desirable spot for a signature on single-signed baseballs.

telephone auction—An auction conducted over the telephone with potential buyers calling in bids rather than physically being present.

Cachet issued to honor the Lou Gehrig stamp in Cooperstown on June 10, 1989 autographed by Ted Williams.

Game-worn White Sox uniform of Ozzie Guillen.

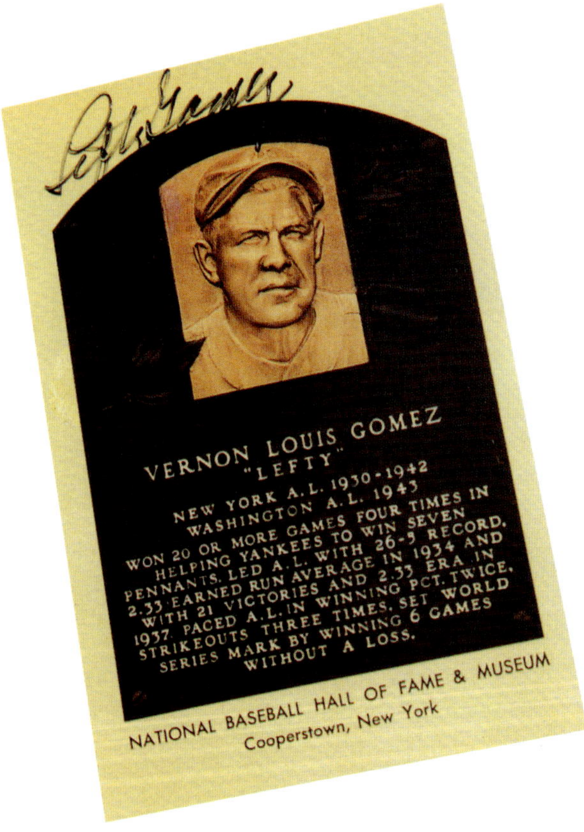

Hall of Fame plaque autographed by Lefty Gomez (d. 1989).

Baseball signed on the "sweet spot" by Stan Musial.

Chapter 10

Culminating Activity

In the world of education, a *culminating activity* usually takes place after all the material is presented and digested and there is a need for a single event that tends to bring everything together with a concise and rewarding conclusion. The twenty-five questions that follow are your culminating activity.

Directions

The questions that follow are not easy. Read each one carefully, reflect, and select the best answer. It is a guarantee that you will miss #25 so no one will secure a perfect score. Do not hesitate to use outside resources in attempting to answer the questions.

1. Which player's autograph is the most difficult to find on a single-signed baseball?
   a. Ken Griffey Jr.
   b. Lou Gehrig
   c. Babe Ruth
2. True or False? Lou Gehrig was a pallbearer at Babe Ruth's funeral.
3. True or False? Adding Hank Aaron's autograph to a single-signed Babe Ruth ball would add to the value of the ball.
4. True or False? Adding Sammy Sosa's signature to a Roger Maris single-signed baseball would diminish the value of the ball.
5. True or False? A 1961 Yankee team-signed baseball and a 1962 Yankee team-signed baseball would have the same approximate value if both were in excellent condition.
6. Which signature below would be considered the rarest?
   a. Babe Ruth
   b. Lou Gehrig
   c. Connie Mack
   d. William Cummings
7. True or False? The Baseball Hall of Fame opened in Cooperstown, N.Y. in 1939.
8. Which autographed baseball has the most value?
   a. Bobby & Barry Bonds
   b. Mickey Mantle and Bobby Murcer
   c. Joe DiMaggio and Ted Williams
   d. John F. Kennedy, Sr.
9. Which autographed baseball has the most value?
   a. 1944 St. Louis Browns
   b. 1958 Brooklyn Dodgers
   c. single-signed Jackie Robinson
   d. single-signed Nolan Ryan
10. True or False? Babe Ruth could have seen Jackie Robinson play in the major leagues.
11. True or False? The rarest of the original Hartland statues is Mickey Mantle.
12. Who could have signed a baseball with a ballpoint pen?
   a. Lou Gehrig
   b. Dizzy Dean
   c. John McGraw
   d. all of the above
   e. none of the above
13. Circle the name of the Hall of Fame member who was inducted first. (5 points total—1 point per correct response)
   - Nellie Fox or Luis Aparicio
   - Pee Wee Reese or Duke Snider
   - Willie Mays or Roy Campanella
   - Bob Feller or Ron Santo
   - Al Barlick or Bill McGowan
14. Who is the only member of the Providence Grays in the Hall of Fame?
15. Which Hall of Fame member below never played in the major leagues?
   a. Herb Pennock
   b. Willie "the Devil" Wells
   c. Goose Goslin
   d. All of the above played in the major leagues
16. Who was the first African-American elected to the Hall of Fame?
17. Which player below is *not* found in a Hartland statue?
   a. Nellie Fox
   b. Eddie Mathews
   c. Derek Jeter
   d. Roger Maris
18. Who is the only New York Met who entered the Hall of Fame as a player?
19. True or False? Ty Cobb played his entire career with Detroit.
20. True or False? A single-signed baseball from Eddie Gaedel of the St. Louis Browns would have more value than a ball signed by Cal Ripken, Jr. or Nolan Ryan.
21. Circle the names of the members of the Hall of Fame below who were pitchers.
   Ernie Lombardi
   Travis Jackson
   Bill Klem
   Ray Schalk
   Sam Crawford
   Arky Vaughan
22. True or False? Dick Groat and Rocky Colavito are both in the Hall of Fame

23. Who is the only man that has been inducted into both the Baseball Hall of Fame and the National Football League Hall of Fame?
24. Which one of the teams below did Babe Ruth *not* play for?
    New York Yankees
    Boston Braves
    St. Louis Browns
    Boston Red Sox
25. What member of the Hall of Fame had his *career* homerun record broken by Babe Ruth?

Scoring Scale
number of points

25—29 Waive the 5-year requirement and go directly to the Hall of Fame
20—24 Your number will be retired at the Social Security Office
15—19 Consider yourself a .275 hitter with no power
0—14 Below the Mendoza Line

Answers: 1. b; 2. F; 3. F; 4. T; 5. F; 6. d; 7. T; 8. d; 9. c; 10. T; 11. F; 12. b; 13. Aparicio, Snider, Feller, Barlick, Campanella; 14. Charles "Old Hoss" Radbourn; 15. Willie Wells; 16. Jackie Robinson; 17. c; 18. Tom Seaver; 19. F; 20. T; 21. none of the men were pitchers; 22. F; 23. Cal Hubbard; 24. c; 25. Roger Connor (132 career homeruns)